A View of the Lake

Living the Dream on Lake Superior

by Beryl Singleton Bissell

Lake Superior Port Cities Inc.

First Edition: June 2011

LAKE SUPERIOR PORT CITIES INC.
P.O. Box 16417
Lake Superior Duluth, Minnesota 55816-0417 USA
Port Cities Inc. 888-BIG LAKE (888-244-5253)

5 4 3 2 1

Library of Congress Cataloging-in-Publication Data

Bissell, Beryl Singleton.
    A view of the lake : living the dream on Lake Superior / by Beryl Singleton Bissell. – 1st ed.
        p. cm.
    ISBN 987-0-942235-74-6
    1. Bissell, Beryl Singleton. 2. Ex-nuns – Biography.
    3. Superior, Lake, Region – Biography. I. Title.
    BX4668.3.B46A3 2011
    277.3'082092–dc22
    [B]   2011003426

Printed in the United States of America

        Editors: Konnie LeMay, Ann Possis
Cover Design: Randy Bauer; photo by Larry & Linda Dunlap
        Printer: Cushing-Malloy Inc., Ann Arbor, Michigan

To my precious husband Bill,
who made all this possible.

Contents

A View
of the Lake

In August 1998, my husband and I made an impulsive move to the North Shore of Lake Superior. We'd fallen in love with a view and bought the property that framed it.

Bill and I were not like other couples who travel to the North Shore at every opportunity and who dream, year after year, of someday owning a home there. It took only two weeks at Norcroft, a writing retreat in Lutsen, to weave my dream. Norcroft legend has it that not only did my husband propose to me while I was there, but that I responded by saying I would marry him ONLY if we moved to the North Shore.

While that's not exactly how it happened, an idyllic two-week vacation at a tiny fisherman's cabin northeast of Grand Marais the following year convinced Bill that "a home on the North Shore" was his dream as well as mine. That winter, without my knowledge, he began to peruse the real estate section of the newspaper for Lake Superior properties. At breakfast one sunny morning in mid-May 1998, Bill looked up from the paper he was reading and asked if I'd like to look at a cabin near Grand Marais. Of course I did! Though the cabin was a bust, the trip was a fateful one. On our way home, a "For Sale by Owner" sign in Schroeder attracted my attention. I suggested that we check it out.

We turned down a very long driveway to find a home that seemed to float on water. "Oh Beryl," Bill said, "I think you've gotten us in deep trouble." The glass front door revealed a house that was filled with windows and those windows were filled with Lake.

The day was one of those spectacular Lake Superior days, with water the color of sapphire, the sun bright, the air clear and warm. The Lake bewitched us. We wanted that property. We reasoned that as long as Bill, an international change management consultant, had access to an airport and phone and fax lines, we could live anywhere we wanted. There was an airport in Duluth and the phone company would supply the phone and fax lines. Before leaving the house that afternoon, we wrote the owner an intent-to-purchase check and drove back to the Cities, exulting.

At home in Arden Hills, reality set in. Neither of us had ever owned such an expensive home, and while the Lake dazzled us, we could not remember what the house looked like.

Our desire to move didn't make sense. We had little experience of the place, knew only its basic attractions – the nearby Boundary Waters, the Superior Hiking Trail and the breathtaking view of Lake Superior. Everything we needed or wanted we had in the Twin Cities: a lovely home, no mortgage, easy access to a major airport, a great arts scene, gourmet dining, bookstores, jazz, theater, friends, children, grandchildren. Moving would also mean that I'd have to give up a job that I loved: associate development director of Milkweed Editions in Minneapolis, one of the finest small literary presses in the nation.

We drew up lists of pros and cons identifying the reasons why we should or should not move. We came up with two pages of reasons to stay where we were. To move, we had only one reason: A view of the Lake.

"If we move, will you promise to finish writing your book?" Bill asked, reminding me that leaving Milkweed might be a good idea. At Milkweed, surrounded by great writing, I'd neglected to work on my own book – a memoir about the search for God that led me into a monastery at the age of 17 and the collapse of that vocation 15 years later in Puerto Rico when I met and fell in love with a priest. Completing the memoir added incentive to our decision-making, yet still we vacillated. At night we'd climb into bed, having decided to forget the whole idea, and the next morning would wake up in a grand funk at the loss of our dream.

The following week we returned to view the property and realized why we couldn't remember what the house looked like. The house was the Lake's homely sister: a nondescript modular home furnished hotel-style with industrial strength carpeting, inexpensive cabinetry and warehouse fluorescent lights. It was, however, spacious and bright, most of its large windows providing a glorious view of Lake Superior.

We spent the day looking at other homes but found nothing that could compare. Nicer homes, yes, but none with five acres of land separating them from the noisy highway. None with charming bridges over runoff creeks. None with an unobstructed view of, and easy access to, Lake Superior.

Despite that convincing return trip, we continued to waffle, torn between the comfort of our lives in the Cities and the unknowns of life on Lake Superior. Unable to reach a decision, I suggested that we put our Arden Hills home on the market. If it sold within two weeks, we were to follow the dream. Knowing my penchant for seeking "signs" when making decisions, Bill agreed. The day we listed the house, we received two offers over and above what we were asking. The universe had spoken.

While blessings preceded our move to Schroeder, trials quickly followed. Days after our arrival, Northwest Airlines – the only carrier flying to and from Duluth at the time – went on strike. That same week, before our phone lines were installed, US West employees also went on strike. Bill's career hung in the balance. Rather than an hour and a half drive to Duluth, it took five hours to reach the Minneapolis airport. Without access to phone lines (cell phones were useless on the North Shore at that time), Bill could not communicate with work when home, nor could he contact me when away. Then too, rather than the quiet terrain we'd envisioned, an energy-processing plant one mile west rumbled day and night, and from the resort to the east the loud voices of reveling campers and screaming children kept us awake at night. Our move suddenly seemed a terrible mistake.

An editorial in the *Cook County News Herald*, commenting on the significant number of people who move to the North Shore to fulfill a dream but leave soon after, spoke directly to us. That night I wrote a proposal for a weekly column based on our experience as North Shore newcomers and sent the editor several sample columns. He liked the idea.

"Newcomer Notes" emerged from the ruminations of a writer who'd arrived on the North Shore having no idea of what life in that place entailed. While focusing first on the trials that beset us after our impulsive move, my columns became more reflective as the Lake became, as it were, my mentor. We'd arrived driving our SUVs, thinking that our only deprivations would be access to nearby groceries and Mr. Movies, but one does not live year-round on Lake Superior without noting the effects lifestyles such as ours have on the environment. Thus it was that Newcomer Notes became a chronicle of how we learned to live on the North Shore, a "we came for the view but we stay because of the place" experience. This memoir emerges from those experiences and from the hundreds of pages of journal notes and daily logs that comprise the essence of our experience. Ours is not a back-to-the-land story. We have running water and electricity and heat our home with propane. It is, rather, a narrative of two ordinary lives transposed into an extraordinary setting where nature and a small community became our teachers: An experience replicated wherever people encounter an environment so profuse with wonders that one wants never again to take them for granted.

This is the place where we came in search of a home and found as well our reason for being.

Seasons
of Learning
Fall

Feeding the Bears

Bill was working in Tennessee during the moving process, so most of the details and the actual move became my responsibility. Moving day logistics complicated matters. The movers, who were to have arrived at 10, didn't arrive until noon. The four employees I'd expected arrived as two. I was distressed, knowing that timing was crucial as the new owner planned to move in later that afternoon. When 3 p.m. arrived and we were still far from finished, I tried to stem a rising sense of panic. A frantic phone call to the moving agency brought the two missing employees to my door, and just in time as it turned out. Our van passed the new owner's truck as it turned the corner onto our block.

I spent the night at a nearby motel on the North Shore and arrived early the next morning to find the movers attempting to back the moving van down our very long driveway. This was not the way the movers preferred to come down driveways, but it was the only way they'd be able to leave. Our driveway did not allow large vans to make U-turns.

Everything Bill and I had managed to merge into my home when we married had followed us north. It took a full day to unload the truck. When the movers finally left, I stood amidst the clutter of unopened boxes and decided to call it quits for the day. Filling the birdfeeders seemed like a more worthwhile endeavor than filling the cupboards. We'd moved for the view, not for the house. Then, having fed the birds, I headed down to the lakeshore to unwind and watch the water. I hugged myself with joy. Our dream had become a reality. Before going to bed that night, I made one last trip outside to view the darkening sky and to listen to the Lake. Above me, myriads of stars swirled in the black night and the Lake gurgled and seethed around its rocks. I would have stayed longer, but as I stood there in the dark, the hair began to rise on the back of my neck. Something or someone was out there with me. Chiding myself for being frightened – this wasn't the Cities after all – I hurried back inside, glad that Bill wasn't there to laugh at my fears.

The next morning, while taking my breakfast down to the ledge rocks to eat – as I was to do often during our first weeks here – I stumbled over a bird feeder. It looked like one that I'd hung the evening before. What was it doing down by the Lake? I looked back at the house to where I'd hung the feeders. The feeding pole dipped crazily toward the lawn and the hanger which I'd attached to the house had disappeared along with all the feeders. My premonition had been right. Something had been out there with me the night before. Most likely a bear.

Having one of the North Shore's larger denizens visit the night I arrived alerted me to the fact that I was not the only owner of the place where we'd moved. And, as if to remind me that this was so, the visitor left a muddy smear on the window in front of my desk. Thrilled but chastened by my first encounter with North Shore wildlife, I left the paw print on the window as a reminder of the bear's visit until heavy rains washed it off the following spring.

For the rest of that summer and fall, I took the feeders in at night. This tactic appeared to work, but eventually I grew careless. Bears have a penchant for letting you know that they've paid a call. Like the bear that visited my first night on the shore, this second one demolished the feeders and left its calling card – another messy paw print on my window.

Those Damned Flies

When the birds flee our northern shore for warmer climates in the fall, a different species of winged creature arrives. Flies. These are not the infamous black flies that invade every spring, leaving the human population speckled with oozing and bloodied bites that torment us for weeks; nor are they the ankle-biting fishflies that arrive in late summer. No, these are the flies that want to share your house during the winter, that littered the window sills and the floors of the empty homes we'd looked at with a real estate agent before committing to this home.

"What do you envision for this house?" the agent piped as we picked our way through one particularly smelly, bug-laden home.

"Getting out of here," I thought. I couldn't envision anything being done with that house, certainly not living there; or, for that matter, spending another minute inside. Sellers would be wise to keep dead flies at a minimum, I thought judgmentally, especially if they want to sell their homes.

I've since discovered that keeping a house fly-free on the North Shore can be an almost impossible task. During the fall, the insect population inside my own home has dipped and peaked with the thermometer, but it has never disappeared despite what I think of as heroic efforts to eliminate every bumbling black visitor. These flies outsmart me every time I open a door. They swarm inside window frames, they darken ledges with their dead bodies, they perform hara-kiri on my kitchen counters. Sometimes I manage to swat several at a time and feel much like the little French tailor who took "seven at one blow." I become a whirling dervish as I swirl around the house waving the vacuum cleaner hose, sucking up the flies as they buzz and swoop around me. All to no avail, it would seem, as the fly population remains steady. Does one fly die? Another immediately takes its place. Warriors of a different sort.

Outside my house, an even thicker population of these flies makes for very happy visitors of another winged sort. The ground, grasses and bushes surrounding us swarm with myriad feathered friends that swoop and spiral after the insects that thrive there. This proliferation of birds would ordinarily be a great opportunity to learn their names, if only I weren't so busy killing the damn flies. I keep my bird book nearby, however, and occasionally take a break from slaughter to try to match the birds I see with the photos in the book. Meanwhile, the birds dine happily outside and don't seem to mind my ongoing ignorance. For their sake I try to welcome the flies.

For the Birds

The Schroeder post office is more than a place to get the mail. Equipped with a coffee pot, candy dish and several chairs, our post office is the spot where the locals meet to greet and gossip.

It was in the Schroeder post office that I met more neighbors in one month than I'd met in five years in Arden Hills. And as often happens in the Schroeder post office, an introduction can lead to a question that leads to more questions. One morning I met Jim Tveekrem who, with his wife, Carol, had tracked migration patterns for the National Bird Banding Laboratory in Laurel, Maryland, for more than 20 years. Jim invited me to come watch.

The morning I acted on that invitation, I saw Jim lifting a tiny redpoll from a gossamer-thin mist net into which I then bungled like an oversized bird. A towering giant of a man, Jim worked with the delicacy of a surgeon, taking care not to injure or frighten the bird as he placed it into a paper bag. As he loosened each bird from the net he identified them for me – a western palm warbler, a song sparrow, a northern water thrush. For someone like me, who'd just started to learn bird identification, his knowledge seemed encyclopedic.

"I think I've got them all," he said. "I'll come back in a bit to check the net again."

Together with Jim I headed to the tent where Carol was banding the birds. She'd just finished banding a yellow-rumped warbler when I entered. I watched as she wetted its tiny head with her middle finger and checked the color of its skull to determine age (faint pink for a young bird, creamier as it ages).

"HY (hatching year)," Carol said. Jim noted that statistic on a clipboard. She then spread its wing and tail feathers and measured them. "Wings. 71.5 millimeters. Tail. 54 millimeters." She blew on its belly. The soft feathers flared briefly then settled. "0 fat."

"Birds build up visible layers of fat to prepare for migrating," Carol explained. "This bird has either stopped to replenish its fat deposits or has not yet begun its journey."

Jim released the warbler into the woods and lifted a yellow-throated vireo, a bird rarely seen this far north, from its bag.

"Doubting bird watchers will want proof," Carol said, laughing softly. "Would you get the camera for me, Jim? It's in the car."

Jim weighed the vireo in its bag, then went to get the camera. While he was gone, I took Jim's place, writing down measurements as Carol called them out. We hadn't quite finished measuring a least flycatcher when Jim returned with the camera.

"Here," Carol said, handing me the flycatcher, "I need you to hold this bird while I get the vireo ready for his portrait."

As the vireo squawked and nipped at Carol's hand and Jim tried to focus the camera, I held the tiny songbird, its head nestled between my trembling index and middle fingers. How warm its body was. I could feel the beating of its heart and in that moment became both captor and protector – the bird so vulnerable in its helplessness and my power as a human so potent.

Greg's Table

Years ago, when my late husband, Vittorio, and I married, my brother Greg gave us a large piece of unfinished mahogany as a wedding gift and prefaced the giving with a lengthy speech about its value – it was "rare, unique and incredible."

Vittorio and I had nodded and smiled and thanked him profusely. Greg was prone to flamboyant exaggeration, but we needed a coffee table and this piece of wood would fill that role nicely. Knowing nothing about wood, we stained it brown and placed it on some cinder blocks. Greg was horrified. It looked terrible.

When Vittorio died of cancer three years later, Greg would periodically remind me of his gift and lament its fate. The mistreated mahogany slab became a rather sad family joke despite my promises to "someday" have something truly beautiful made from it. I hauled it from house to house as I moved. It came north with Bill and me and was relegated to the garage as I pondered what to do with it. Greg had died the year before we moved, and I felt badly that he'd never had the joy of seeing that piece of mahogany turned into something beautiful as I'd promised.

I thought of Greg the afternoon I drove past a "Woodworking" sign and decided to follow the arrow pointing to a workshop. Al Evenson, who'd moved north to retire but found himself busier than ever, was dubious. A single piece of mahogany in such dimensions was rare. It was too large for a single slab. Nevertheless, my description piqued his interest and he agreed to take a look.

On my next trip to Grand Marais, I took the piece of mahogany with me and showed it to Al. When he verified that, yes, it was mahogany, I told him of my dream: a meditation table – low, long and elegant – to front our living room picture window, a table that would reflect the beauty of the Lake beyond that window.

When Al delivered the finished table to our home, he'd transformed the scarred and stained mahogany slab. It floated above luminescent birch rails, the soft pinkish glow of the birch a stunning contrast with the burnished radiance of the mahogany top. Al used trimmings from the slab to make slender mahogany and walnut legs and connected them with pegged mortise and tenon joints to the rails. I could almost hear Greg exult over this transformation.

"Oh, my God!" he'd say. "This table is almost as beautiful as a woman's body." Greg's long-ago wedding gift had assumed a form that reflected the spirit of the man who gave it. Every morning as I sit next to this table to meditate, I think of Greg and offer a prayer of thanksgiving. I don't need the table to remember my brother, but somehow, this table has returned his voice.

Bob Silver's Tree

Our purchase of a North Shore home stirred up a miller's brew of reactions from our acquaintances. Relatives and friends frothed over the "biggest mistake" of our lives and business contacts threw up their hands and cried "crazy." Artists, poets and writers, on the other hand, were unanimous in their approval. Their eyes revealed their longing. We had accomplished that of which they'd only dreamed.

Our home has lots of room for guests and we often have visitors. The North Shore in late summer and early fall makes converts even of those who doubted our sanity when we bought this place. As November approaches, our full-house syndrome reverses, with only the hardier breed of guest arriving to share our cold. While a number of Schroeder residents take off at the first signs of November, heading for homes in Arizona or Florida, there are many older residents who actually prefer to stay year-round. One such hardy elder was the late Bob Silver who, when I met him, was 85 years old and claimed that while he might not be the oldest, he was definitely "the longest lived resident of Schroeder."

When I moved to Schroeder, I had a nearsighted perspective of the area. The Lake and its immediate environs occupied my attention, not the hills on the other side of the highway, nor the residents who lived there. Until Bob sent me a message via the postmaster to "Stop in and say hello," I didn't know he existed, nor had I noticed his big lumber shed situated just a bit west of our home on the other side of the highway.

I found Bob in a back room of the shed, where he'd run the Cross River Lumber Company until he retired at age 80. He was building his Patio Perfect rustic outdoor cedar furniture. Dressed in tattered coveralls to keep his immaculate flannel shirt and wool pants clean, Bob was busy shaping a cedar bough when I entered. Pale amber light washed the inside of the shed, bathing the old barrel woodstove and tool-laden workbenches in sepia tones, making me feel as if I'd just stepped inside a history book.

"I was hoping you'd stop by," he said, thus beginning what would become one of my most treasured friendships. I was to spend many an afternoon with Bob in his unheated office – me bundled in a heavy jacket, hat and mittens, Bob wearing only a simple wool sweater over his flannel shirt. He claimed to be plenty warm.

"All you need is some woolen underwear, a good wool shirt, wool pants and sweater," he told me, smiling at my incredulity.

From the time he was a small boy, Bob had collected stories about the town's past, its people, history and folklore and had become, because of his knowledge, an unofficial town and area historian who loved sharing those stories. During our first visit, he'd shown me his father's old logging map, a much-worn hand-drawn chart marking the locations of the Cross River dams. Until then, I'd not known that the Cross River had been used by the John Schroeder Lumber Company around the turn of the century to hurl old-growth timber into Lake Superior to be towed to Ashland, Wisconsin, for milling. From his desk drawer, he'd then pulled a faded picture he'd taken 40 years earlier of a huge yellow birch growing from a fallen white pine.

"Counted more than 300 rings on that pine; birch at least 130 years. How long before the birch began to grow over that pine is anybody's guess," he said shaking his head, as if still amazed at that wonder. Bob had another wonder he wanted to show me: a strangely shaped piece of wood that looked like an ornate column spiraling toward the roof of his shed. "Vine strangled the life right out of that tree," Bob muttered. And indeed it had, the vine entwining itself so tightly around the maple that the maple had assumed the shape of the vine. Where the maple forked, a slight indentation in the strangling vine formed the eye of a snake. Bob was forever surprising me. He'd call me up to tell me to come see the largest puffball he'd ever encountered or a deer antler not devoured by animals but covered with moss or to tell me the number of vehicles per minute he'd counted passing by on Highway 61 that morning during fall color season.

Sometimes Bob would show up at my house with an old book on logging, or a manuscript he'd written on the Schroeder Tote Road. I'd make a cup of tea, Felix our cat would snuggle onto Bob's lap, and he'd talk about his plans to write the history of the Pork Bay trail, one of the earliest trails into the area, or would launch into another narrative of happenings both strange and wonderful that he'd witnessed. Bob could quote from memory the exact section of a survey map where other families had lived when he was growing up. He could recite the names of all their children, what they did for a living, when they died, and where they moved. But Bob was amazingly reticent about himself. Only when it involved a good story – such as having unwittingly come across the fittings for the A-bomb while repairing a door on a building on the Pacific Island of Tinian, or the time he took his axe to a cedar and a hibernating bear charged out from under that tree – did he mention himself.

There were times when this focus on the factual frustrated me. I wanted more personal anecdotes. "What was a typical day like for you as a young boy growing up in the woods?" I'd ask, and he'd tell me about the Alger Smith Company Railroad and Joe Cramer's store next to the grade. If you wanted to know about Bob, you had to ask others.

Bob, the most honest and kindly man I ever knew, died in February 2002. Others would tell me that Bob "never uttered a falsehood or said something negative about another person." No wonder Bob was able to say that he'd always been well treated in Schroeder. "Never had a bad experience," he said. In living the adage "Do unto others as you would have them do unto you," Bob had elicited a similar commitment from the community in which he lived.

My Lakeshore Monster

Lurking off our lakeshore property is a monster that appeared one day soon after we'd moved to Schroeder.

Lake Superior was unusually quiet the day I first met our Nessie, barely a ripple across its satin surface. I was sitting on a fallen birch enjoying the sun and the seemingly unending expanse of blue sky and water when a swooshing gurgle startled me. I looked up in time to see a shining black shape emerge from the Lake, water cascading off its back and pooling around its flanks before sinking back under the surface of the Lake.

I soon realized that my monster was only a submerged Lake boulder, but I've developed a real fondness for Nessie, as I've called her these many years. Her visits, which are sporadic when the Lake is at average height, become familiar as levels drop during the winter. Come spring, before the melt turns rivers into floods that raise the water level, migrating ducks land on Nessie's broad back.

There's an eagle that sometimes hangs around our lakeshore, selecting a dead birch as a preferred roosting spot before lofting toward the monster rock, hovering over it with a great swelling of wings before dropping onto its humped surface to guzzle water. The eagle reminds me of a heavy drinker tossing back hard liquor.

When new people arrive to visit, Nessie's sudden appearance never fails to startle them. "Did you see that?" they ask, certain that they are the first to spot this aberrance of the Lake's surface. Some have grown so familiar with Nessie's ongoing presence that they inquire about her well-being from afar. There have been seasons of drought, however, when Nessie could not hide even if she wanted to.

One winter, we'd not only acquired a new beach (prompting my husband to quip that if the Lake continued to drop we'll have six rather than five acres of land), but Nessie's back grew so wide that an entire flock of migrating ducks settled on it to rest.

There's a rocky point between our property and our neighbor's land that periodically donates sections of its ledge to the Lake. If I'm correct, and the point drops another really big rock, Nessie might one day have a sister to keep her company.

Buntings and Bows

In the fall and spring, songbirds, raptors, ducks and geese spiral along Lake Superior, a major avian migration flyway. Tiny warblers soar from cleared areas into the trees where they hop upward from one branch to another and send the bushes shuddering. Juncos and sparrows peck busily on the gravel roads. Canadian geese, mergansers, and goldeneyes ply the Lake. The snow buntings, however, are the most persistent familiars in fall.

The first time I saw the swirling dance of the snow buntings, I thought they resembled white ribbons and bows. They appear so joyful, but their seeming preference for socializing on roads puzzles and worries me. One day, as I drove up the Sawbill Trail, the snow buntings' predilection for roads, cars and danger seemed excessive. Congregating on the road, they'd scatter upward as my car approached, only to land a bit farther ahead of me. It felt like a dance. Scatter, land, scatter, land.

"This is no way to avoid impact, little friends," I thought to myself as I slowed the car to a mere crawl; yet the small avian creatures, chirping and twirling, continued to whirl in front of me. I'd almost despaired of the buntings leaving, when they suddenly banked to the left and flew up into the white spruces lining the road.

While I didn't kill any snow buntings on that trip, a little red squirrel wasn't so lucky. I saw it flash in front of me, heard the thump and gasped as I watched it spasm and tumble on the road until it stopped quivering and lay still. Uncertain what to do, I pulled over. Should I take it to an animal rehabilitator if it was still alive? Or – too awful to even think about (save that I did) – drive over it again to end its agony? I got out of the car and checked, much relieved to find it already dead. Hating to leave it there on the road for further destruction, I rolled the little creature onto a pine bough and laid it among the roadside grasses. Even the jolly little snow buntings that accompanied me again on my way home failed to ease my sense of guilt. I'd never been responsible for the death of anything larger than a mouse, save vicariously through the young male cat we'd adopted. Felix had quickly diminished the size of what had been, until then, an ever-increasing brood of chipmunks.

Felix must have wondered at my renewed vigilance when I returned home that evening. "No more killing," I told him, "Neither you nor me."

Unable to stalk the outside of the house, Felix sat in front of our window meowing, chittering, twitching and leaping. Frustrated at his inability to seize a bird, he turned his attention to the myriad cluster flies that buzzed above him. He'd lunge, capture one, down it with his paw and eat it. He snapped vigorously at flies with my blessing.

A Man and
His Cat

"Full-figured female. Won't last long. Act fast." read the
description of Ellie, a female cat of mixed lineage, housed in
Duluth's Animal Shelter and awaiting a home.

When I proposed getting another cat, Bill wasn't certain he was
ready. He was still mourning the loss of Felix, the Russian Blue
who'd come to us via the shelter in St. Cloud the month we'd
moved in. When Felix died suddenly of congestive heart failure
barely two years after we adopted him, I hadn't planned on
replacing him so quickly. Certainly not within three months of his
death when an envelope arrived from a friend with a clipping of a
"pet of the week" ad and a cryptic note asking: "Is there a cat in
your future?"

Ellie's photo, showing a fat and bug-eyed dark gray cat,
touched me. Despite the ad's admonition to "act fast," I learned on
getting her that Ellie had been waiting for someone to "act fast" for
more than three months. She was 5 years old.

I've heard that cats can suffer from depression and this seems
plausible because when we first got Ellie she was much different
from the frisky Felix who had pranced into our hearts two years
earlier. Ellie wasn't interested in play, nor did she groom herself. She
spent most of every day sleeping. It took me several weeks to get all
the mats out of her fur and to eliminate its sticky feel; several more
weeks before she began to groom herself. It took Ellie longer to
learn how to play.

Bill, who'd been immediately smitten by Ellie's charms, made
teaching her to play his special mission. When Bill first sent a laser

beam skittering across the rug, she'd watch from her mat but wouldn't move. It took a more threatening game to get her to respond: Growling. This elicited at first something between a mewl and rumble in the back of her throat, but she still refused to budge. More growling. She'd rise from her perch on the couch and do that back-of-the-throat thing. It took more growling from Bill before she'd leap off the couch and hurtle downstairs where she'd crouch, waiting for Bill. Eventually, Ellie began to initiate games, lurking at the foot of the stairs and meowing for Bill, then flying off with a great thudding of paws to hide under the bed or recliner. She even started to galumph through the house on her own (which is how fat cats run), galloping up and down the hallway in the middle of the night or thundering up the stairs to check on visitors at the front door.

One day, Ellie decided to follow us down to the Lake, picking her way across the rocky beach with obvious displeasure. The crows kicked up a ruckus, dive-bombing our waddling lady, not realizing that she was too fat to pose a threat to their young. We waited as she inched her way up inclines – belly swaying, tail trying to stay erect but faltering with the effort – stopping occasionally to lie down, forcing us to rest with her. However, as soon as we rose, so did she, moving on with only an occasional protesting meow.

Ellie became Bill's cat. When he was off on business, I did my best to play, but Ellie's eyes would take on a distant look and, with a disgusted swipe of her tail, she'd depart. Nor could I carry her through the house as did Bill, with one arm. At 16 pounds she was too heavy. Bill could carry her in the crook of his arm, her head balanced in his palm, from window to window so she could chitter and slaver at birds, chipmunks and red squirrels she saw outside. Though Ellie was on a lose-weight diet from the day we got her, she remained a steady 16 pounds. An unwilling dieter, she'd head frequently to her feeding bowl in a hopeless quest to find something there, having devoured her small scoop of Science Diet Light the minute it hit the bowl.

One night around a year into Ellie's adoption as member of our family, my friend Brigitte and I watched Bill take her for a nighttime walk on the lakeshore. Although his white sweater was easy to detect, Ellie was just a fat shadow rolling after him in the dark.

"A man and his cat," Brigitte commented, and I laughed in agreement.

Camping and
Kayaks

On a late Thursday afternoon in September 1999, I dragged my sleeping bag out from under the badminton net in the garage, half expecting to find a nest of small rodents tucked within its crumpled folds. I hadn't used that bag in years.

At the urging of my new friend Mary, whom I'd met in a class on North Shore authors, I'd enrolled in a weekend course "in pursuit of physical activities in the natural world." Hanging the sleeping bag over the deck to air, I wondered what I'd gotten myself into. While I congratulated myself for being willing to try a sport I'd never before attempted, kayaking, I wasn't sure about the tenting. Not only did I not have a tent of my own, I hated tenting. Although I'd done Boundary Waters Outward Bound in my late 50s, a Montana rafting trip on the Yellowstone River soon after Bill and I married convinced me that tents and I were a poor match. The pup tent that Bill and I were assigned was so small that, when in it, I turned into the wicked witch of the west. Not even Bill's wacky sense of humor could lift me from that tenting funk. I was relieved when Mary said she had an extra tent I could use. At least I'd have a space of my own in which to get nasty.

On the morning the course began, Mary picked me up in her new blue Subaru. Sitting jauntily atop the Subaru was the bright blue kayak she had just finished building at the North House Folk School in Grand Marais, and above that kayak was one of the bluest skies I'd ever seen. After days of fog, the change in weather elated me. I could do anything in weather like this. I could even sleep in a tent and learn to kayak.

Before our first kayaking session near Brimson, Minnesota, Kathleen Devereaux, a women's spirituality therapist and group member, offered a traditional Anishinaabe (Ojibway) gift of prayers and tobacco. Mary, who was taking her kayak into the water for the first time, launched first. We whooped and hollered congratulations when it stayed afloat and laughed when Mary waved her paddle in triumph. Next to launch were the advanced kayakers. We beginners launched last.

"Wear your kayak like a skin," Kathleen advised. I tried to envision the kayak as my skin, but when we headed out Greenwood Lake turned choppy. By the time we'd reached the other side, we were battling small whitecaps, and flying spray coursed down my glasses. I found it difficult to hug the kayak with my knees, but I actually liked the slight edge of fear the waves induced, the challenge of staying balanced and controlling the movement of the kayak. When, after lunch, we returned again to our kayaks, the wind had died down. Paddling across a now tranquil lake, I discovered that I'd actually grown quite comfortable in this new skin.

That night, following a sauna and dip in the icy water, I headed back to my camp where, sheltered only slightly from the brilliance of a full moon and a temperature that was rapidly dropping toward freezing, I realized that I was quite content in my little tent as well.

Newcomers

How long does it take to claim a place as home? Not long. How long does it take to become a local? Forever.

Having finally found "home," I'd hoped that within a few years I'd no longer be considered a newcomer. A letter to the editor disabused me of this fantasy. Although the writer, who'd been born and raised on the North Shore, did not say so directly, Bill and I were among the newcomers whose presence made it impossible for him to live here. He wanted to return but could not afford a home.

I understood his anger. Like him, I'd grown up in an area where property values have so escalated that Bill and I could never afford to buy a home there. I remember returning to my childhood home as a young adult and feeling sick at heart. Palatial houses had sprouted from the fields where I had played. Oak and maple woodlands had been pillaged to make way for swaths of green lawns and decorative landscaping. I was outraged that what was once mine was no longer available to me. I looked at those homes and attached a label to their inhabitants: Outsiders. I resented every one of them.

I felt the same sickness sweep over me while reviewing the 1998-99 winter issue of *Minnesota History*. On page 159, a "Map of Indian Land Cessions and Reservations" painted a vivid portrait of what it means to lose a home. For centuries before the arrival of the white man, the Anishinaabe-Ojibway people had hunted and fished the Arrowhead region, and before them, for at least 8,000 years, so had other tribes. I had known these facts, but what I hadn't recognized, and what this map revealed so clearly, was the speed with which Ojibway were pressured from their lands and the inequity of the treaties that opened this area to settlement. Within the space of two years after the signing of the Treaty of La Pointe in 1854, most of northern Minnesota was ceded to white men, the portion allotted to the tribes measly specks on the map.

"[A map] is only paper and ink," writes Beryl Markham in her famous memoir *West with the Night*, "but if you think a little, if you pause a moment, you will see that these two things have seldom joined to make a document so modest and yet so full with histories of hope or sagas of conquest."

Maps illustrating stories of hope and conquest make it impossible to avoid what such charts show so clearly. We are here because others are gone. We come in search of place and dislodge those who were here before us. Few of us can claim to be truly native.

"If anything can claim to possess this place, surely it is they (the boulders), who have lain here for centuries," wrote Minnesota author Paul Gruchow.

While we might think of place as ours, the land itself is the only true native. We are but fleeting passers-by.

Historical Society

The photos on the wall of a local café fascinated me. A meat wagon and horses, a one-room schoolhouse with children lined up in front, a fisherman's picnic, a father and son cutting ice on Dyer's Lake, fishermen with boxes of freshly salted herring, a hunter standing with wolf hides. Pasted on each photo, neatly typed on yellowing strips of paper, were the names of the people and places in the pictures.

I studied these photos as I ate, wondering what their lives had been like. The opportunity to become part of this local history arose during one of my daily jaunts up our driveway to the post office when I learned that Schroeder has its own historical society.

That a township of 180 some people should have its own historical society so tickled me that I joined the same day, even offering to help in whatever way I could. I didn't realize how quickly the Schroeder Area Historical Society would take me up on my offer. Within days, I discovered that I'd been appointed chair of the Oral History and Marketing and Publicity Committees. And I wasn't even on the board!

Suddenly, as Oral History chair, I found myself awash in the names of the descendants of people whose pictures I'd seen in the café. For weeks my mind teetered beneath the weight of family trees laden with descendants of the original settlers to this area – all of whom seemed to be related to my neighbors.

The committee of advisors I gathered were infinitely patient. My address book grew fat with names and addresses. Attached to each were cryptic notes: "Now living in Florida, but returns in summer. Father was a fisherman. Sister might still be alive. Interview this summer. Related to so-and-so who is also related to so-and-so. Priority 1."

As I struggled to develop my list of people to interview, the calendar dropped days like over-ripe berries. I wondered how best to convince these old-time residents that I could be trusted with their stories. I wished that someone had done this years earlier when time was not so critical, when the first settlers were still alive and their children were not aging so rapidly. I wanted the people on my list to become more than names, their experiences, their dreams, their wisdom an essential part of community folklore from which future generations can draw. The stories I gathered during those interviews would later provide material for the Schroeder Area Historical Society's 2010 book, *Schroeder Area History ... as Shared by Those Who Lived It*.

I couldn't have chosen a better way to become part of a community than collecting these oral histories. Rather than being referred to only as "that newcomer," I was invited into the homes of longtime residents to share tea, gather stories and look at family albums. Word spread that I was seeking stories. One morning during this process, my neighbor Kevin Johnson knocked at my door and offered me a small gray binder. Inside were the neatly typed memories of one of Schroeder's early residents, Jeanne, the young French war bride that Ray Parent brought to Schroeder in 1919. As I began to read, my excitement kept pace. Inside this manuscript were stories of her husband's illegal hunting activities in which she was sometimes an unwilling participant. Such as the time her hubby told the Department of Natural Resources deputy trying to nab him that his wife, lying blanket-covered in bed, was very ill, though actually she was quite healthy. Under the blanket with Jeanne was a heap of illegal pelts her husband had hidden there.

The oral histories I recorded and helped to transcribe cannot, however, fill the gap left by the unrecorded lives of those who have died. We can speak authentically only of what we ourselves have experienced. Oral histories, for this reason, focus on first-person recollections. Children cannot tell their parents' stories. Only those parents, writing about or recording what life was like for them, can share their personal histories. A common longing shared during these interviews by second-generation descendants refers to this loss.

"I wish I had kept their letters. I wish I had recorded their stories" were words I heard repeatedly. There were times when, as I sat taping others' memories, I experienced this loss personally. My mother died before I was wise enough to ask questions. I now hold only fragments of her life, each piece bristling with questions, each piece weighted with the unknown.

We are born. We die. We do what others do. Some of the elders I interviewed wondered why I wanted to know about their lives when they'd been so uneventful. In the telling, they came to a fresh appreciation of themselves and the community in which they'd lived such a long time. Like a musical score played over and over again, the sound, timing and interpretation are never quite the same.

Natural Settings

One of the benefits of having been appointed marketing and PR chair for the historical society was the opportunity to meet and interview the speakers for our programs. The first such interview I held was with Betty Powell Skoog, the author of *A Life in Two Worlds*, republished in 2010 by the Schroeder Area Historical Society – a memoir about growing up in the Ojibway tradition on a remote homestead on Lake Saganagons, Ontario. Preferring to meet in person, Betty had invited me to her home in Finland, just off Highway 1.

The drive to Betty's home was picture-postcard beautiful, especially when I turned off Highway 61 to take Highway 1 into the hills. Both sides of that amazing, curving road were bordered with flaming banks of vermilion, scarlet and gold. By the time I arrived at Betty's immaculate little home, with its rich green lawn, neat garden patches flush with hardy vegetables and pots and trellises cascading with flowers, I was bewitched. Betty's home seemed to have stepped straight from a fairy tale.

Betty had prepared coffee and cookies, which she served in the gazebo on her deck. As we chatted, I could hear the rush of water. "Do you have a stream running through your property?" I asked.

"Come and see," said Betty, leading me to the edge of the cliff on which her home stood. I gasped. Below us the Baptism River appeared to rush straight at the cliff on which Betty's house stood. It hurled itself at the solid rock as if determined to break through before making a sharp turn at the foot of the cliff and racing off in a southwesterly direction toward Lake Superior.

Betty and her husband, Ken, had recently returned from a trip to Betty's childhood home of Lake Saganagons after a lapse of 42 years. A small cadre of freelance writers and photographers followed them into the wilderness to document their return. Betty spread photos of this trip on the dining room table. "The trip was wonderful," Betty told me, "but I almost felt like an alien returning home. I was born free there and the woods were my playgrounds. Now there are so many rules and regulations about access. In addition, other things have changed. All the big pines are gone." She pointed to a picture of her standing in the doorway of a small cabin. "I built that little cabin with my sister Jeanette when I was 12 years old, so we could practice our music without disturbing our grandparents. It's still standing."

"Did your grandfather help you?" I asked. Betty answered that she and Jeanette had built it themselves. Their grandfather had given them the skills with which to build it.

"Two beavers have built a home there and added a beautiful little pond to the original homestead," she said, smiling at the memory. Betty liked to think that her beloved grandparents had returned as those beavers to live again where they'd once lived so happily.

Aquayweasheik, her Ojibway grandmother, and Jack Powell, her Irish grandfather, gave Betty the skills necessary to live in the wilderness. But, believing she would grow up to be a trapper, they did not send her away to school. Instead her grandfather taught her all he knew of reading and writing, and she taught herself the rest.

Although Betty said that she was glad she didn't go to a boarding school where she would have missed the love and support of her mother and grandparents, she'd felt her lack of education keenly at times, especially when trying to get jobs. This lack of schooling, however, makes her accomplishments even more noteworthy. Without the benefit of a formal education, Betty has successfully negotiated life between two very different civilizations and published a charming account of this journey for posterity.

Death on the River

When I first moved to Schroeder, a dilapidated sign next to the Cross River Falls warned hikers to stay off its rocks. "People have died here," it threatened. I'd smiled at that sign, wondering how those falls could be dangerous when they looked rather benevolent, the water streaming over them in narrow silver threads. I didn't know then how furiously the water could rush over those descending rocks in the spring or after a heavy rain. When I arrived in Schroeder, a dry summer was drawing to a close and the falls had shrunk to a mere trickle.

The nearby Temperance River can also appear non-threatening … not in its gorges which thunder continuously, but in its dark pools. While snowmelt and spring rains turn the Cross and Temperance into raging torrents, one sunny day after another in late summer can give the rivers a deceptively benevolent appearance. The Temperance, despite its mild sounding name, has claimed six lives since I've lived here. Locals often swim in its inviting pools, but they know what to look for. Outsiders and tourists, on the other hand, remain naively innocent of the danger. A heavy rainfall upriver can create errant currents, drop water temperature and raise water levels. I was forcibly reminded of this threat the day in September 2000 that we took Bill's parents for a cruise up Lake Superior on the *Grampa Woo III*.

It was a day made for such a cruise – the Lake tranquil and cobalt blue, the hills just starting to flame, the sun brilliant in a cloudless sky. Two little boys hung over the boat's railing, viewing the water, the spray sending a fine mist over their faces. "Might I take their photos?" I asked their father. He agreed, and the boys obligingly pushed the brims of their baseball caps toward the back of their heads so I could see their faces better.

"The youngest one reminds me of the toddler I took care of yesterday," a woman standing next to me said. "Mother came screaming to me, asking if I'd watch him."

The story was tragic: The father had drowned in the Temperance saving his 8-year-old son. When the boy was pulled from the river alive, he was suffering from hypothermia. His mother needed someone to watch her toddler while she accompanied him to the hospital. That death bore an eerie similarity to the drowning in the Temperance the year before – a father who died while trying to save his 12-year-old daughter. The fathers saved their children, but, though both were said to have been excellent swimmers, they could not save themselves.

In 2001, a 22-year-old man fell into the river while climbing a cliff. In June 2008, the Temperance swept a 17-year-old camper and a 29-year-old counselor to their deaths. In July 2009, a 45-year-old man swimming in the Temperance got caught in a current and drowned.

There is a campground next to our home. Camping parents with young children often explore our ledgerock lakeshore. They have a wonderful cobble beach on which to play and gather agates, but the ledgerock holds a powerful attraction. We felt the same attraction when we moved here, so I understand when children are drawn to it. When I see children alone on the rocks and no adults with them, I get upset. Neither the children nor their parents seem to realize how slippery those rocks can be, how suddenly waves can rise to cover those rocks, how little time before hypothermia sets in.

I remember especially a 5-year-old in a red sweatshirt and his little sister with curly blond hair who ran down those slippery rocks toward the waves screaming, "Come on waves! Just try to catch me. You just try." While they obeyed me when I told them not to play on the ledgerock without their parents present, I should have asked them where their parents were and taken them back there myself.

As I photographed the small boys aboard the *Grampa Woo III* that September afternoon, I wished them good parents, long lives and many a happy and safe return to Lake Superior.

Waging War on Thistles

In late summer and early fall, Bill wages a war on the thistles that flourish among the lupine and tall grasses alongside our driveway. He pulls their thorny stems from the earth and burns their flowers, yet every year they seem to multiply. Bill seems to be losing the war, for even as he eradicates the thistles on our property, entire plantations of new thistle sprout along Highway 61 and send their seeds back onto our land.

I've helped Bill fight the thistles and know what a thorny, painful and frustrating job it can be. I count myself lucky when Bill dons his heavy gloves and heads up the driveway to fight his war without telling me. Each time he sights a new patch of the thorny monsters peeking from behind a shrub or woodpile, frustration and resignation wage their own war within him. Eradication means little in thistle world. They bloom full grown where yesterday Bill slaughtered them all. He has been thorough, tenacious and determined in his extermination program, yet the thistles refuse to be cowed.

Bill uses the technique his dad taught him as a farm boy in Iowa, what the University of Minnesota Extension website calls "mechanical" means for controlling bull and musk thistle: hand-pulling. He continues to use this method, rather than the other method suggested for thistle control – spraying with herbicides like Stinger and Banvel or 2, 4-D – because we live next to the Lake and everything we use on the soil eventually makes its way back into Lake Superior.

Several years ago I read an article by David James Duncan in which he spoke of the individual's role in helping to heal the natural world. Rather than focusing on worldwide problems, which can be overwhelming and leave one feeling hopeless, he suggested lovingly caring for what I think he termed "our own bit of the river." He was referring, of course, to more than rivers. He meant our own backyards and neighborhoods.

Though I often find myself wringing my hands about the global environmental issues confronting us – fearful for future generations who will endure the fallout from our rapacious use of the planet – I find comfort believing that Duncan is right, that we can change the world one backyard and neighborhood at a time. When it comes to ridding the landscape of thistles and other exotics, however, this change will most likely involve many an ongoing skirmish and plenty of backyard wars.

A Night
in the Woods

When hiking the Superior Hiking Trail at 6 in the morning, Bill and I rarely encounter other hikers. But one cool September dawn in 2003, Bill and I saw a solitary woman on the trail ahead of us. For the sake of this story, we'll call her Donna.

Donna was not hiking for pleasure as we were. She was looking for her friend Dave, a fellow volunteer in charge of a campsite on that section of trail. She told us that they'd driven from Duluth after work the night before to check its condition and clean it up if necessary. While Dave went to clean the campsite, Donna, who'd dislocated her knee a few days earlier, waited in the truck.

Believing he'd be back before dark, Dave left wearing only a light jacket and carrying a rake and plastic bag. When dark fell, and Dave had still not returned, Donna comforted herself by reasoning that he was a seasoned outdoorsman and had probably decided to spend the night in camp. He'd return at first light, she thought. In time to get to work.

When dawn arrived and Dave had still not returned, Donna went in search of him. We met her when she was still around a mile from the campsite he'd gone to clean. Bill ran ahead to check the campsite to see if Dave was there. When that proved futile, Donna suggested that perhaps Dave had gone on to clean the next campsite. "He's strong," she insisted. "He knows these woods." Though Donna thought Dave would be upset if we went for help, Bill ran back to the trailhead to do just that.

Meanwhile, Donna and I continued on toward the next campsite. We'd reached the place where the Superior Hiking Trail crosses the old logging Schroeder Tote Road, when we heard Bill shouting. "I found Dave," he shouted triumphantly. "Don't go any farther."

Dave had been overtaken by dark on a night with no moon and, unable to navigate by stars because of the heavy tree canopy, he'd been forced to spend a very cold damp night in the woods. At dawn, by following a brook downstream, Dave eventually located the trailhead, but found Donna gone. Knowing she was probably looking for him, he'd headed back into the woods to find her when Bill encountered him. Exhausted by his ordeal, he'd returned to his truck to wait.

Donna's knee was by then giving her a lot of pain. I suggested that Bill return to our car and find Harry Johnson who lived off the Tote Road. Harry had an ATV that could negotiate the badly rutted and rocky trail. When Harry arrived, he looked more like a rescuing knight than a guy on an ATV wearing flannels. Donna climbed behind him and I followed the ATV on foot back to where Bill and Dave waited for us on the paved road. After a hot shower and hot breakfast, Dave acknowledged that he'd made some poor judgment calls. He'd forgotten about the shortened days.

I hate to think how far Dave and Donna might have walked, trying to find one another. Had Donna continued on to the next campsite, she'd have encountered some very difficult terrain. And, while Dave would eventually have caught up with her, getting back to the truck would have been an ordeal.

Lesson learned. Even seasoned hikers need a plan B should plan A fail … and in the North Woods, it very likely will.

Gulls of Longing

The herring gulls swooped toward the slight figure which, buffeted by wind and rain, stood calling them. They rose, one phalanx after another, from their distant island and swirled into a white vortex above the steel gray waters of Lake Superior. I held an umbrella over my friend Virginia's head as the wind whipped her silvery hair and the gulls soared toward her.

"So lovely to see you again," she cried, opening her arms wide as the gulls screeched and wheeled above us. From the bag of scraps she'd brought with her, Virginia plucked bits and pieces of bread, chicken, cookies and pie. Following the momentum of Virginia's arm, the gulls circled and grabbed. They scurried around our feet, pecking, snatching and gobbling. Virginia laughed and clapped her hands. "I'm home again!" she cried.

Eight months earlier Virginia had sold her lakeside home in Lutsen – where she'd once encountered a bear as it teetered on her narrow balcony, where red and gray foxes romped, and a flying squirrel entertained her at night – to move to a residence for seniors. At the residence, pine siskins and gold finches and hummingbirds no longer visited; window feeders were not permitted. Neither were cats or dogs. Virginia always had cats. Virginia was the friend who'd sent me the ad about Ellie, asking if there was a cat in our future. She missed her cats terribly. The hallways in her residence were so empty that Virginia once threatened to dance naked through them. "I just can't make myself believe that living in this apartment is all that is left of my life," she told me.

As I stood with Virginia among the swirling cloud of gulls, I felt her loss. In a residence, she'd been deprived of all that made life as brilliantly hued as the quilts she sewed. There was sadness in the humor that had her confessing: "I've been reduced to watching every damn wedding and funeral that happens across the street." We waited until the gulls had devoured every last crumb, then turned and walked back through the rain to the car.

During the years that followed the sale of her home, Virginia moved from residence to residence, seeking a place where she'd feel comfortable. I'd take her on drives into the hills, and on every drive she'd point out some spot from which we could view the Lake and say, "Someday, I'm going to buy a small lot like that and live there. A shack would do."

Virginia was still living in her lovely Lutsen home when I met her for the first time. After introducing me to her cats, she'd taken me on a tour of her house, showing with special delight its upper story dedicated to quilt making. Virginia used her walls the way an artist works at an easel – to create, to observe from a distance, to complete a work of art. Unfinished quilts in every color of the rainbow hung on every available wall. Magazines featuring quilts shared space with piles of fabric. Rulers and scissors and strips and pieces of cut fabric covered tables and chairs.

One quilt drew my attention. Composed of thousands of tiny pieces of fabric cut in squares, diamonds and triangles, it contained every shade and hue of blue imaginable in every possible pattern: paisleys, ferns, stars, flowers, shimmers, swirls, feathers, dots, loops and swirling vines. It was exquisite. I told her I'd be interested in buying that quilt when it was finished.

"I never sell my quilts," she'd snapped. "I give them to my friends." I said nothing more about the quilt and she never mentioned it until the day she called to tell me she had a surprise.

"For your birthday," she said smiling, handing me the beautiful blue quilt.

Virginia died in 2009 still dreaming of a place of her own back among the society of trees and wild living things she so loved. This quilt adorns our bed, a constant reminder of the indomitable woman who taught me about flowers and back roads and longing and friendship.

Seasons of Learning
Winter

The Seven
Dancing Sisters

City lights, streetlights, floodlights and houselights sear the
night skies over heavily populated areas the world over, making
stargazing a thing of dreams. But here on Minnesota's North Shore,
the darkness can be so intense that the stars seem to multiply. Even
children notice the difference. When my granddaughter Amber was
8, she once asked why we had more stars here than they had at their
home in Owatonna.

On nights of no moon, the dark can be so intense it renders
one blind. The first time I encountered such dark, I was in my
writing shed at Norcroft and lost track of time. It was close to
midnight when I tried to find my way back to the lodge. It was so
black out – no moon at all – that I had to feel my way to the house
with my feet and ears. As I shuffled along, trying to ensure that my
sneakers kept contact with the gravel driveway, listening for the
crunch of the crushed rocks under my feet, I mourned the
flashlight I'd left in my room. What did I know about such dark? I
was a North Shore neophyte.

Bill and I often sit in the dark in our living room, watching the
night sky and its effect on the Lake. Sometimes, especially in
winter, stars can appear in such abundance that I simply have to
view them in the out-of-doors. Early in my life here, I took a class
on stars and night skies. Every night I'd head outside with my
book on the constellations and a flashlight, the lens covered with
red construction paper so as not to interfere with stargazing
trying to learn my way around the night skies. One night, Sirius
(I'm not joking) took over my education. He beckoned to me.

He had something to share. I could almost hear what he was saying.

"Look. Over there. There's Orion. He's trying to impress you with his belt and club. And that guy in his chariot? The one with those goats on his shoulder? That's Auriga. He'd like to ditch the goats but can't find any takers. You can ignore Perseus; he's too caught up in himself as it is, flexing his muscles like that. No, feast your eyes instead a bit below. Would you look at the Pleiades sisters! By Pluto, those girls can dance!"

I turned my eyes in the direction Sirius pointed and sure enough, it did look like the Pleiades were dancing. How else to explain the movement I saw there? The Pleiades sparked one after the other, leaping forward and spinning back to allow another to flaunt her beauty. I even thought I saw silver threads spin from one sister to the other as they danced and twirled. Such a show provided for free! Not a penny expended for such beauty. Just a bit of dark.

When Bill and I traveled through British Columbia several years ago, we stayed at the Observatory B&B in Osoyoos. The astronomer who owned that B&B took us to the top of the house where a moving dome housed three huge telescopes. That night he showed us, through those telescopes, the Hercules cluster, the Whirlpool galaxy and Andromeda. Though we were impressed, he wished for darker skies. "It's not dark enough here for really good viewing," he said. That was why he and other amateur astronomers were investing in a swath of land in Arizona where they could build homes far enough from civilization to ensure as little artificial light as possible breaks their darkness.

I wondered if our night skies would meet with his approval.

North Shore Neighborliness

Whenever Bill and I travel in winter, kind neighbors undertake the task of watching our home to make sure the pipes don't freeze. When Bob Silver was alive, our home survived one of winter's worst temperature dips without event because we had the foresight to entrust it to his excellent care.

One of Bob's mottos was "if you need something, build it yourself." Bob didn't trust the Honeywell Winter Watchman we'd installed (a timer-like contraption that turns on a light if the temperature inside the house drops below a certain point). He made something he could rely on – a wooden stand on which he'd placed a basic indoor thermometer placed next to the door's window so he could verify the inside temperature without having to continually enter the house. "A constant 54 degrees" he told us when we returned.

Bob took "checking on" to a "caring for" level, something that reflects what I have come to think of as the North Shore's special brand of neighborliness. It's a gift that I see reflected in the time people take with one another, the sharing, the openness, the personal concern. It's what makes friends like Jan call us in Puerto Rico to tell us our roof had just blown off in a storm but not to worry, she'd gotten Pete down to make temporary repairs that should hold until the rain stops.

Perhaps the small size of our community makes neighborliness visible, but since moving here I've become much more aware of what the word "neighbor" means. When I arrived in Schroeder, I was a pilgrim on a journey. Until then I'd remained aloof from community involvement. I'd excused my behavior by claiming that I was a single mother, working full time while trying to complete my education and taking care of a sick mother. The truth was that even if I'd had the time, energy and knowledge, I would not have gotten involved. I'd always made a concerted effort to avoid anything that smacked of "togetherness" unless it involved my children. Schroeder changed that.

Perhaps it was the neighbors who welcomed us into their midst. On the other hand, maybe it was Schroeder's unique history – a composite of heroic efforts to survive in a remote and harshly beautiful environment. Most likely it was community need. In a small community like this, the "someone else" I used to rely on to pick up the slack does not exist. "Someone else" is not heard much around here. Most of us realize that if we don't, who will perform the tasks that help create a vital, lively community?

I sometimes joke that North Shore volunteers run the place. While that's an exaggeration, the generosity and enthusiasm of volunteers keep the community humming. In view of all this giving, that little stand that Bob built for our house was not just a temperature monitor for the weather. It was a gauge reflecting the soul of this community.

Grand Portage Passage

The North Shore abounds in dogsledding fans: those who attend the races and those who raise and race those dogsled dogs. Never having been to such a race, I was excited to learn that the first annual Grand Portage Passage race was looking for volunteers. When I called to offer my help, the race had already started but I was told that the folks at Devil Track Lake, a six-hour stopover location, could use all the help they could get.

I arrived early that evening, intent on being there when the action started. As the lodge was offering a buffet for the volunteers, and knowing no one, I asked to join a table with two empty seats. Nick, one of the two men already seated at the table, introduced himself. He'd traveled to Grand Portage from Green Bay, Wisconsin, to help out and was one of the nine volunteer veterinarians there to perform mandatory checks on the dogs. Jim Brick, the other person at the table, was also a veterinarian. He'd traveled to the race from Grove City, Ohio, explaining that they were there to monitor the dogs for fatigue, sore muscles and injuries and to pull them from the race if they suffered from any of these signs. "This race is all about maximizing care of the dogs," he said.

"And you?" Nick asked.

"I'm a volunteer but have no idea what I can do to help. I've never done this before. Have no experience."

"You don't need experience," he laughed. "There are all sorts of jobs you could do. Road crossings need an especially large number of volunteers."

Jim described a road crossing – the shadowy whisper of sleds that fly silently from the woods and across the road where volunteers wait with hot drinks and a blazing fire. When the vets excused themselves to prepare for the expected dogs, I headed back outside as well. Seeing a small figure busy shoveling snow next to a handling truck, I asked if this was where the dogs bed down? Eleven-year old Dallas Seavey stopped shoveling and cocked his head. "Sure is ma'am. We're building a trench to keep them out of the wind." I was about to suggest that I help when his 14-year-old brother, Tyrell, came up and asked for the shovel.

"Got to dig an opening so the dogs can get through." Dallas shrugged and yielded the shovel. While waiting for its return, he told me that his dad was Mitch Seavey from Sterling, Alaska. "We expect him to be the first musher to arrive at this checkpoint." Dallas's 16-year-old brother, Danny, was also racing his own team. Dallas then pointed to a man who hadn't stopped shoveling since I arrived. "That's my granddad," he beamed. "Ran the first Iditarod in 1973 and again in 1974. Ran the 25th race in 1997."

Certain he saw his dad's team approaching, Dallas excused himself and ran toward the lake. A light bobbed in the distance, a silent wave moving swiftly toward us across the ice-covered lake. I arrived at the checkpoint just as the dogs, muzzles sporting icy whiskers, arrived. One dog, in the middle, howled; the rest stood quietly while handlers removed their booties. The dogs were much smaller and thinner than I'd imagined. I'd expected big huskies like the teams I'd seen in movies. When I mentioned this to the man next to me, he said that these dogs were bred for endurance and were actually faster and stronger than larger dogs.

I followed Dallas as he led the dogs toward the trench he'd helped dig and layered with straw as bedding. Tyrell tethered the dogs and Dallas began distributing a small amount of food to them.

"Is that all they get?" I asked.

"Oh no." Dallas said, laughing. "The vets have to check them first. After that they'll get loads of food – meat and fish mixed in warm water." Some of the dogs had already settled down to rest, while others turned in tight circles, padding at the straw before snuggling down. The dogs were lying under blankets and waiting for the vets when I moved back to the lodge to see if there was anything there with which I could help. Learning that there wasn't, and feeling that I was in the way, I left.

The next year, I shared a late-night road crossing with my kayaking friend Mary. Though no one stopped for hot drinks or breaks, the night was as magical as the vets had said it would be, the moon a thin sliver that cast long shadows over the snow. Mary and I stomped about, keeping the fire blazing and our feet warm, waiting for the sleds, hearing only the whisper of the runners on the snow and the panting of the dogs as the sleds whipped past.

Bill and I have attended several races since then, once bringing our grandchildren to Grand Portage Lodge for the start of the race. Amber had broken her leg so we pulled her across the snow on a sled and settled her near the starting point. She had a close-up view of the yelping, barking dogs, some of which jumped straight up into the air in their desire to run. The contrast between the teams taking off and those yet to run was stunning: Absolute silence as opposed to the excited racket of the waiting dogs. The running dogs focused on only one thing, the race itself.

Shrike Attack

One winter morning, while gazing at Lake Superior from our living room window, I saw a downward spiral of white breast from the suet feeder and thought a hairy woodpecker must have lost its balance.

I smiled at such apparent clumsiness in a bird, not realizing I'd witnessed a shrike attack. The first time I'd seen a shrike, I thought what a jolly plump fellow he looked. He was easy to see, sitting immobile on the birch above our feeders. My birding book identified the black masked eyes, the curved black beak as that of the northern shrike – eater of songbirds, impaler of prey. I knew then why the songbirds had disappeared from my feeder.

The next day I watched as the shrike seized two small mice browsing midst fallen seeds. Later I saw the shrike tearing and ripping at something on a thorn branch. When it flew away, that something dangled from its beak.

Winter focuses a harsher light on North Shore living, reminding me that nature, while beautiful, caters to no one and no thing; beauty is not always benevolent.

Winter, however, holds happier markings. On a perfect winter day filled with sun and sky, I went snowshoeing up Le Veaux Mountain and interrupted a tiny red squirrel having lunch. He'd chosen a bright patch of sunlight in which to dine and was obviously not expecting guests, for he scampered away as soon as he heard me coming. Not wanting to intrude on his meal, I stopped as soon as I saw him. He, in turn, stopped scurrying. Perhaps he thought the intruder had disappeared or had suddenly been transformed into a shrub because instead of scuttling up a tree to scold me, it took him only a second to turn around and hurry back to his lunch – a partially eaten spruce cone only a few inches from my boot. He soon settled back to dining, folding his tail up and over his back like a warm jacket, nibbling daintily – elbows tucked in and holding the cone in a manner of which even Emily Post would have approved.

If you've ever attended a red squirrel's feast, you've observed the amazing shelling technique that allows it to cast aside the used casings even as it chews the miniscule kernels within. Having never witnessed such an event, I stayed until he finished – around four minutes to complete his meal. Then off he scooted, zigzagging first to the left and then to the right before plunging his nose into the snow. After some snuffling about and several changes in direction, he plowed his way into a hole and disappeared. I waited until I was certain he wasn't going to return before examining the midden he'd left behind. Either the cone had no spine or he had eaten even that, for all I could find were the thin lavender-hued petals of the cone on which he'd dined.

The squirrel's disappearance into the snow puzzled me. Was I mistaken in thinking squirrels lived in trees, slept tucked into pockets of leaves, twigs and moss made cozy with bits of Kleenex, fur and feathers? I scanned my growing collection of nature books and discovered in Mark Stensaas' *Canoe Country Wildlife* that this red squirrel did indeed live in a tree and that when he stuck his nose in the snow he was probably trying to locate a nearby storage locker by scent. Hidden in a hollow log or stump to keep the cones from drying, this larder might have been near the hole into which I'd seen him disappear. Red squirrels, according to Stensaas, have been known to secret as many as 14,000 cones and mushrooms within their feeding territory. Ignorant of Little Red's prolific gathering skills, I'd gathered a pocketful of cones while snowshoeing and on my return left them where I'd seen the squirrel. Perhaps they'd induce him to dine in front of some other lucky traveler on snowshoes.

A Sense of Home

On a Friday evening in February of our first year on the shore, my husband, Bill, caught me off guard as he slumped, exhausted, at the dinner table.

"I think buying a home on the North Shore might have been a mistake," he said.

This was not the light-hearted banter Bill makes when, for example, we arrive at the Duluth airport (after rising at 3 a.m.) to find his flight has been cancelled because of fog. This remark came from the depths. Bill had pneumonia.

Bill didn't get pneumonia at home in Schroeder. He got it in Houston, where he and many of his clients came down with a vicious version of the flu. Bill, however, was the only victim whose flu morphed into pneumonia. The stress of commuting to work from the North Shore looked like it might undo our dream. Not even the most beautiful vista imaginable – Lake Superior shimmering in the winter light – could help Bill's perspective that night.

While I lived in paradise, Bill slogged through purgatory. Seven days a week I saw the Lake, hiked the woods and viewed the wildlife. For five days every week, Bill lived out of a suitcase, slept and ate in hotels and fought the germs circulating through polluted air vents in airplanes and offices. Buying a home in heaven had burdened him. Bill also missed city life, the culture, theater, concerts, museums and excitement. While I'd found "home" here immediately, Bill had not. At home so seldom and for such short periods of time, he didn't even know where to find the sugar or the frying pan.

Bill's discouragement caused me to ponder the differences in our experiences of life on Lake Superior. What was it, I wondered, that brought a sense of belonging to place? Was it the time we spend there? The way we live there? Was it a growing knowledge and love of our surroundings? An understanding of the community? Was it something we can make happen, or was it more tenuous, a gift?

I concluded that it was most likely a combination of all of the above. It could also be the simple act of tuning into WTIP, our very own public radio station, and listening to a fun-filled pledge drive asking for freshly caught mice for Archimedes, a rescued screech owl, complete with premium – an Archimedes' pellet.

Bill and I have lived on Lake Superior for 12 years. During that time, at least once a year, Bill has talked about moving. It took a winter sojourn in Florida, in 2009 – six months of condominium living – for Bill to realize that Lake Superior really was home. We returned with a sense of relief. Florida was noisy – traffic, leaf blowers, lawn mowers, horns, sirens and helicopters. Loud voices, televisions with volume turned high, music blaring up from the poolside. It was crowded and possessed some of the most dangerous drivers I've ever seen. We've driven in Puerto Rico, where Bill is convinced no one has ever taken a driving lesson, and in Italy, which abounds in breakneck, sidewalk-leaping drivers, but Florida drivers were as bad if not worse.

Bill's commitment to this place has grown to such a degree that this year, 12 years after we bought the house, we finally got rid of the industrial carpet we'd promised ourselves we'd dispose of as soon as we moved in. In addition, the sliding glass doors that yawned over a 20-foot abyss for 12 years now open onto a beautiful deck with an even better view of the Lake. Wood floors, new kitchen cabinets and six-paneled maple doors complete the picture. We attached the old kitchen cabinets to the walls in the furnace room and were able to recycle everything else, offering the carpet, old doors and kitchen appliances for free on the electronic community bulletin board. Everything was claimed within minutes.

This year, though Bill's schedule remains as hectic as ever, he has not once mentioned wanting to move. Instead, whenever he mentions the house, it is always as "our beautiful home."

Northern Lights

I'd been living on the North Shore for well over a year but had never seen the northern lights. Local gift shops and galleries featured representations of local artists' sightings of the phenomenon. An oil painting of white pines and northern lights hung in our living room. I'd had visitors who, on their first trip to see us, had driven through "shimmering green blankets" of light. But though I'd checked our night skies repeatedly, I'd never seen the real thing. I'd come to think that northern lights couldn't be seen where we lived on the lakeshore, that one needed to live in the hills facing north to observe the lights.

On the winter morning I first saw the northern lights, I rose before dawn to stretch and pray as I usually do. I laid my sticky pad on the floor, stood and faced the Lake, breathed deeply and, focusing my eyes on the horizon for balance, noticed that the sky looked strange. I looked more closely and realized that the sky was streaked from horizon to dome with shimmering streamers of light. Were these *the* lights? I wasn't certain because they had little color. Ditching the breathing exercises, I hurried outside and looked until I was certain that the platinum and silver waves above me were actually northern lights. Then I bounded into the bedroom to wake Bill. Together we rushed out into the sub-zero temperatures dressed only in our pajamas and robes. Together we stood on the deck and entered ground zero of an incredible light show that shuddered around us like fireworks behind gauzy veils. It rippled and spun and folded; it expanded and dissolved; it burst and flared. I felt a searing joy.

While the lights were still streaming, I left Bill on the deck and called Virginia, my elderly quilting friend who'd moved to a senior residence. We'd made a pact to call one another, no matter what the hour, should we spot the northern lights. Virginia picked the phone up immediately. She'd been awake for more than two hours trying to decide whether or not to call me, she said. From where she lived, reflected light from the town made it difficult to discern whether the pulsing lights she'd observed were the real thing. In Schroeder's darkness Bill and I could see the northern lights more clearly.

Bill recently called me from the Northwest Territories, where he was working, to tell me that he and his fellow consultants had just traveled by dogsled into the Arctic night to view the northern lights up close. His voice trembled with feeling. "Reds, greens, blues. We laughed like children. We cried for joy. It was unbelievable." His emotion, while describing the scene, was as raw as the Arctic night in which he stood.

Cross River Snowshoes

"Have you ever snowshoed the Cross River?" Kevin Johnson asked one day during our first winter on the shore. The thought of trudging upriver on snowshoes frightened me. A neighbor had recently fallen into that river on his snowmobile, his disappearance causing an all-out search and rescue operation in Schroeder.

Kevin smiled at my concern. "There's a big difference between the weight of a snowmobile and the weight of a human," he told me. "Four feet of snow and ice could easily support us if you are interested in checking out some gorgeous winter scenes." When he mentioned that he planned to take his 6-year-old son Jesse, I relaxed. If Jesse came, snowshoeing the Cross River had to be safe.

I sat behind Kevin on his snowmobile while Bill and Jesse teetered on the back of the sled carrying our poles and shoes. The snow was so deep that soon after leaving the Schroeder Tote Road the snowmobile bogged down and could go no farther. We donned our snowshoes and hiked the rest of the way to the river, following the tracks of a moose going the same direction. The river was a track-lovers paradise. Kevin pointed out the trough made by an otter as it coasted down the snow into the dark icy pools under the ice. Embedded in those tracks were those of a wolf. Either the wolf was too late or the otter too smart, because there were no signs of attack.

Other traces of animal life were not as hopeful. In several places swirling stripes marked the snow where tiny vole prints disappeared. An owl perhaps. Whatever had captured those creatures left plenty more for the pine martens and foxes, considering the number of tracks surrounding us.

Trekking with Kevin I did not have to puzzle over signs of which I was unsure. Kevin knew these animals. He'd grown up here and his family was among the North Shore's earliest settlers. Bill and I confidently followed him as he zigzagged back and forth across the river, seeking the safest passage, warning us away from the telltale indentations that signaled holes in the ice cover. After hiking for an hour, Jesse began to tire. Recently recovered from a serious virus, this tenacious little boy plodded along as far as he could before complaining. Bill and I decided to continue on our own, but the farther we moved up river, the more my confidence drained away. By the time we reached the hiking trail bridge, I was ready to turn around. The roar of the water under our feet had become unnerving and each time Bill (who led the way) sank into the snow, I tensed.

On the way back, Bill's foot hit a real hole. Luckily his snowshoe was bigger than the hole was wide and he was able to bridge it, but his shouted warning scared me. I tripped on my snowshoes and fell. We'd been hiking along a steep ice ledge, with the river churning dark and menacing on our left. Now my entire body tipped in that direction. Even as I told myself to stay calm, I heard myself screaming. Would the ice support my efforts to get up or would I continue to slide toward the river? Heart pounding and filled with fury at my clumsiness and our foolhardiness, I struggled back to my feet and swore that the Cross River would be off-limits for the rest of the season. Twelve years later, it remains that way.

A Night of
Shooting Stars

Entering the Earth's atmosphere at speeds of more than 158,000 miles per hour, the Leonids are extremely fast meteors that leave long, fiery trails behind them. While Leonid meteor showers occur annually, every 33 years, when the Earth whirls through the dense cloud of meteoric dust left by a close encounter with comet Temple-Tuttle, mankind is treated to an especially dazzling meteor display. In 1833, it was estimated that more than 100,000 and possibly as many as 200,000 meteors had streaked through the night sky, a fireworks display unlike any other.

When I learned that on November 19, 2002, between 1,000 and 2,000 meteors per hour were predicted to flash through the predawn sky, I set my alarm clock for 4:30 that morning when the Leonid display was to peak in our area. I planned to watch the peak through the large picture window in our living room, seated in a comfortable easy chair. This window faces east, the suggested direction for viewing the fiery nighttime display. A good plan considering the hour. Unfortunately clouds obscured the night sky from my window. To watch the Leonids, I would have to enter the night in front of the house, where there were no clouds and no large windows through which to view them.

It took me longer to dress than I'd hoped because I'd just had surgery on my left hand, but though I missed five minutes of peak display, I entered a night iridescent with wonder. The moon, partially obscured by trees, etched trembling shadows across our snow-covered driveway. Stars seemed to fly as clouds scudded across the sky. Gazing intently into the dark, I saw a thin flash of light, then another, and another. Soon the night was threaded with silvery fish, streaking in all directions. I turned with the clouds from east to west. Even in that direction the meteors played tag. Some of these flaming streaks flashed yellow and green before disappearing. One seemed to sport a reddish head.

There were so many meteors and my neck got so tired from craning upward, that I decided to lie down on the driveway. So what if there might be wolves nearby. So what if on the ground I'd look more like prey than human. I wanted to stay for the whole wondrous show and flat on my back was definitely the best position.

Small, vulnerable and intensely alive at that moment, I gave thanks for the incredible universe that sustains and enlivens all creatures. I was no longer sipping from the cup of life, I'd become one with it.

January is Death

On January 14, 2000, I drove to Minneapolis to say goodbye to a dear friend who was unconscious and dying … a friend so angry with me that he'd not notified me when he moved back to Minnesota from California and who had not let me know that he was dying.

During the four hours it took to drive from Schroeder to Minneapolis, I pondered what I would say when I entered Phil's hospital room. Perhaps I'd simply take his hand and tell him how terribly sad I was about his dying. I'd apologize for allowing a rift in our friendship. I would read some of his favorite poetry to him, reminisce about the laughter we'd shared. I'd thank him for being the charismatic and inspiring professor who'd changed my life by telling me I was a writer.

My friend Deanna, who'd stayed close to Phil, was with me. Deanna had been the one to tell me he was dying. She suggested we go together to see Phil before he died. I felt profound gratitude for her offer. We met at her home north of the Cities and left from there to drive to the hospital. Deanna's presence was a godsend, especially when we found Phil's hospital bed empty, his room vacant and awaiting the next patient. Phil had died only hours before we got there. Our trip to say goodbye had failed.

While driving home, trying to come to terms with Phil's death and our unresolved conflict, I heard Garrison Keillor reflect that in January we don't just think of death. "January *is* death," he stated.

I find this true. January is a hard month in the Northland, a month of bitter cold and frozen septic systems and bursting pipes.

A month when both predator and prey die of starvation. When ice storms crack and kill trees and freeze chickadees in their nest holes. My first husband, Vittorio, died in January, as did my dear friend Sandra, as did Phil. Yet if January is death, it is also gift.

I read somewhere that we don't really learn to live until we begin to die. That the price of life is death. Death reminds us to cherish life. I remember the gratitude with which Vittorio and I greeted each dawn during his illness; the hope and expectations that my friend Sandra brought to her final days. I don't know if Phil, in his final days, felt the same way. As long as I'd known him he'd continued to smoke heavily and to ignore his worsening diabetes. When confronted, he'd told me that he wanted to die but his multiple trips to hospital emergency rooms and intensive care units with heart issues seemed to prove otherwise. Like my brother Greg, who told me that if he'd known he'd live so long he'd have taken better care of his health, Phil might have treated his body more kindly had he known that he'd die while still quite young. Had I known that I would lose my friend Phil without reconciling or saying goodbye, I would have taken better care of our friendship.

The rift that separated us was born of a misunderstanding easily rectified if I'd made an effort to understand why he'd taken offense. Regrets, however, are of little use to anyone. It's what we do with those regrets, what we learn from our mistakes, that make them such painful but needful gifts. At Phil's memorial luncheon, I thanked Phil publicly for the inspiration he'd brought to so many lives but I wished I'd been able to tell him in person.

Whenever January comes round with its anniversaries of loss, I think of the loved ones who have moved on. I remember to honor life for the gratuitous gift it is and to treasure friendship as one of its shining jewels.

Learning to Ski

I've never been graceful. I'm as clumsy now as I was when a 10-year-old. I still manage to bump into walls and to trip on air. Neither am I particularly fond of heights. Terrified, is more like it. For this reason, I stayed clear of the Lutsen Ski Hills until my kayaking, dog-mushing friend Mary gave me a 60th birthday gift of a "free lesson and full day on the slopes." I could no longer avoid those hills.

And so it was that on a sunny day in March, I found myself walking duck-footed up the bunny hill and plowing to the bottom for what seemed like hours. When ski instructor Jack told me it was time to hit the towrope, I sighed and gritted my teeth. Hanging onto a towrope wasn't inviting nor was the towrope itself, icy and strung as it was alongside a drop-off.

"Just lean back in your boots," Jack said when I told him I'd been having trouble with my shoulders. "Let the rope do the work." I did as he said, and the process worked fine until the child in front of me got tangled in his skis and fell down. I'd be joining him in a minute, I thought.

"Let the rope slide through your hands!" a woman yelled. Having no other option, I let the rope slide as she said, and, wonder of wonders, did not collide with the child nor did I slide backward down the hill as I'd feared. The woman, presumably the child's mother, lifted him bodily and reattached him to the rope. We continued upward. What would happen when I let go of the rope? The skis were not extensions of my body, they were weighted foreigners designed to slide ... away from me.

"Bend those knees. Lean forward. Shin against boot." Jack barked as I tottered off the rope. I leaned forward, pressed shin against boot and the skis straightened.

"Follow me," he instructed, and I did, opening and closing the skis and moving downhill so slowly that, at times, I rolled to a stop.

"Eyes on those mountains," Jack commanded. I yanked my eyes from my skis where I'd locked them when we began the descent. "Keep those arms in position. No wings." I tucked my elbows next to my waist. "Pretend you're holding a tray."

I was concentrating on holding that imaginary tray when a gaggle of 5-year-olds lurched into my path. I plowed to another stop. When I finally reached the bottom of the hill, I was ready for a break. Certainly we'd been at this for more than an hour. I was wrong. Up we went again. Then down. We did this repeatedly. The skis were beginning to feel good. I swerved between cones. I skied faster and managed to spray a bit of snow on my final descent. I was ready for a real ski hill. Proudly, I skied to the lift, rode confidently to the top of the easiest hill and made it to the bottom still standing. When I finally got home, I called Bill in Buenos Aires, where he was working, and told him the news.

"Good for you," he said. "When I lived in Colorado the newspapers were always printing stories about 70- and 80-year-olds taking their first lesson."

"But I'm only 60," I interjected.

"Just as newsworthy," he replied, laughing. I could almost hear him smile across the miles.

I'd like to say that I've since haunted the slopes in winter, but the only skiing I've done has been on cross-country trails. At my age, I explain, it's too easy to break bones. Besides, a cross-country ski pass is a lot cheaper than a day on the slopes.

Something Will
Eat It

When snow falls, deer leave the hills to seek asylum on the lakeshore, but die by the score as they try to cross Highway 61.

The snow falls heavier in the hills than on the lakeshore. In the hills, wolves have the advantage. Their wide and furry paws act like snowshoes. Sharp-hooved deer flounder in deep snow. When deer leave the hills for the lakeshore, they must cross Highway 61. In winter the waysides are littered with deer carcasses and automobile body shops do a ripping business.

"Do you know what to do when a deer runs in front of your car?" Pat the postmaster asked me when I was a very new newcomer.

"Sure! Brake or try to avoid it." I answered.

"That's the worst thing you can do," he said. "Braking can cause an accident. Swerving will dump you into a ditch. See a deer and hit the gas pedal hard and fast. Better a dead deer than a dead you."

I don't know about you, but I don't normally speed up when I encounter something on the road. I brake. I swerve. I stop. I was on my way home from Duluth, taking extra care because it was night and icy, staying within the speed limit, scanning the ditches for the reflective lights that often signify the presence of deer when I hit a deer. Until then I'd been certain that by driving carefully anyone could avoid hitting a deer. Deer were, after all, much larger than the small squirrel I'd killed. Even at night one should be able to spot them. Right?

Wrong. I did not see the young doe that leaped from a ditch in front of my car. Acting reflexively, I did everything I'd been warned not to do. I braked and I swerved. The car shuddered and slowed, sliding several hundred feet across the Little Manitou River Bridge before I had it back under control. I pulled to the side of the road, my hands trembling and heart pounding. The headlights of the vehicle behind me backlit a dark shape wobbling on the highway. The truck stopped. A young man leaned out of its window. "Are you all right?" he shouted.

"Yes. I'm fine. But what about the deer. Did you see it?"

"It's alive. Lurching around," he said. My stomach sank. The image of the red squirrel flooded my mind. Its contorted agony. Better to have killed the deer than to have hurt it badly.

"The important thing is that you're OK," he said.

"But what if it's badly injured?"

"I'll go back and check on it. If it's in bad shape, I'll try to find something to kill it." He jumped from the truck and began rooting around in the back of his truck. Although hunting season was over, I hoped he had a gun in his truck. In a daze I followed him back to the deer which had managed to cross the highway. The young man's flashlight illumined the deer. I could see her large ears poking from among the bushes, her face toward us.

"I'm so sorry, so sorry," I called to the deer, hoping she could hear me, as if an apology would do any good. Dead deer were the products of careless drivers, truckers going too fast to slow down, not people like me who drove with special care.

"It's lying down," the young man said, "but it's not going to let me get near it." I was relieved that he wasn't going to try to bludgeon the poor creature to death. All he had was his large flashlight.

"Something will kill and eat it. It's nature's way," he said. We stood there for a few moments. The deer didn't move. I could see her luminous eyes in the glare of the flashlight. There was no accusation in them, no grieving, only wary alertness. This was the wild after all, and I was a predator.

The next morning, as I tried to tape my parking light (which was dangling like an eye torn from its socket) back into the front fender, a futile hope rose within me. There were no signs of blood on the car, no other signs of impact, only a gaping hole in the plastic cover of the headlamp and a bit of fur trapped in the handle of the passenger side door. Perhaps "my" deer would survive like the two lame deer who'd showed up at our house for feeding several years in a row.

Baby, It's Cold Outside

Forty-some years ago, before the advent of patches, gum, acupuncture and the like to assist those trying to quit smoking, my four-pack-a-day friend Nina decided to ditch the habit.

Going cold turkey didn't work. Nina succeeded when she began tricking herself. She pretended she was not quitting; she was merely delaying gratification. Nina began waiting five minutes before lighting her second cigarette. Successful with five-minute intervals between cigarettes, she slowly increased the time until she'd spaced her cigarettes to eight-hour intervals. Finally down to one cigarette a day, she decided she didn't need it and quit for good.

I remembered Nina's efforts when Bill and I went snowshoeing on a particularly cold day. The sun was bright, but the temperature was minus 11 degrees Fahrenheit. My fingers, victims of the circulation problem known as Raynaud's Syndrome, went numb and turned waxen in color almost immediately. No matter how I tried to get circulation back, my fingers stayed frozen. Bill encouraged me to move faster to force the circulation back into my hands, but nothing happened. They remained bloodless and painful.

I was frustrated with my weakness, angry that my hands might force us to return early to the car. I hated ruining a great outing for Bill, who worked so hard during the week and had only one day to relax. The pain in my hands was so great, however, that it matched the agony I'd experienced when I smashed the fingers of my right hand in the garage door. Bill turned to check my progress and saw the pain in my eyes.

"Beryl, we can turn back," he said, his voice so filled with caring, so free of accusation, that I felt instantly relieved. Bill wanted me to be safe. Knowing we could turn back if my hands didn't improve, I was able to tell him that I wanted to keep going as long as I could. Like Nina and her cigarettes, I could push on for five minutes, 10, 20, knowing we could always turn back. With that realization I stopped tensing and ceased whimpering.

When I was a young widow in New Jersey, I'd thought of moving back to Puerto Rico where I'd lived as a teenager and where my mother was still living. If not Puerto Rico, some state farther south. I wanted warmth. Not winter. Instead I moved north. To Minnesota. The children and I arrived in Minnesota in the midst of an Alberta Clipper. Subzero temperatures prevailed and snow piled in six- and seven-foot drifts around the Blaine home into which we'd moved. I'd never been so cold. My teeth chattered, my body tensed, and my toes turned to ice. Within weeks I'd developed the symptoms of Raynaud's, the fingers of both my right and left hands losing their circulation and doing their best to play dead. By the end of that winter, however, I'd grown hardier. I no longer trembled with the cold, though my hands remained vulnerable. The Raynaud's had not abated. For 17 years, while living in the Minneapolis/St. Paul area, my feelings about winter vacillated. I endured winter, grew stronger in the cold; sometimes I even liked it, but I never loved it.

And then we moved even farther north rather than heading south. Here on Lake Superior, I fell in love with winter. Perhaps it's the winter sports I began to enjoy here, the snowshoeing and cross-country skiing. Maybe it's the wonder of a wild lakeshore wrapped in winter, hills blanketed with snow, steam rising like smoky geysers from the Lake as the cold air drops onto the warmer water. Perhaps it's the animals that show themselves in such abundance during winter – deer, wolves, bald eagles and ravens, the tracks of tiny scurrying creatures.

Though snow-laden winters are no longer what they once were, I continue to love winter here. Instead of thinking "Oh no, winter" as I once did when the temperatures began to drop, I now feel a surge of joy when winter reappears. I look at Lake Superior and laugh. When winter arrives, Lake Superior takes over where Nina left off … smoking.

Deer Yard

When we bought our home in Schroeder, the former owner suggested that we feed the deer; so we did. Feeding the deer that first winter was lovely; come spring, however, the deer, besides eating what we provided, began to prune every living bush and shrub on the property. They even nibbled at the spruce seedlings that we were told they didn't eat. That summer, one doe that had flourished on Bill's largess the winter before decided that my hostas and daylily buds were meant for her dining pleasure. No amount of shouting or pot banging could discourage her. Before I'd enjoyed a single bloom, she'd harvested the entire crop.

During our second winter, I told Bill that we ought not to feed the deer. The DNR discourages feeding deer. Besides, if we did not feed the deer, perhaps they'd stay on the other side of the highway. Perhaps my hostas would survive the next summer. I reminded him about the deer who'd died at the head of our driveway a month earlier. That deer had remained untouched by scavengers for almost two weeks. When Bill flew home from work in Argentina, he'd had to hack into that body (with much retching and gagging) to entice the scavengers to dine.

"But they come anyway. Deer always come during winter," he reasoned. He was right. Deer had been hanging out in our woods ever since we'd arrived, even before we began feeding them. What Bill didn't mention was the growth of our deer population. The first deer to arrive were the scouts; they'd hung around doing typical deerlike things: pulling at grass, ripping at shrubs, and flying off – tails raised high – at any sign of movement. This was just a ruse.

They had an ulterior motive. They wanted to disarm us into thinking we could easily feed a few deer. Meanwhile, they sent word to all the other deer in the neighborhood: "Hey, guys. Check out this place. The food is great. And there's lots of it." That had to be how it happened; how we ended up feeding 60 deer.

For three weeks of subzero temperatures during our second winter, I held firm, refusing to acknowledge the deer, strengthening my resolve by reminding myself that they'd eaten my garden. I stood firm even when a particularly pushy doe (probably the one who'd eaten my hostas) got right in my face, gazing soulfully at me only inches from the window where I wrote. Then one day I made the mistake of leaving Bill alone in the house to confront those accusing eyes. I returned home to find our detached garage filled with 90-pound sacks of deer feed and 15 bales of alfalfa.

Bill's excused his profligacy by reminding me that the grandchildren were coming for Christmas and they LOVED feeding the deer. Several weeks before the grandkids arrived, Bill began to forge his route. Bill's trail led from the garage through the center of the front yard, then down around the back of the house and up across the bridge and into the woods. He wanted the children to see the deer from every window in the house.

When the grandchildren arrived that Christmas, 5-year-old Amber followed Bill as he fed the deer. She had her own little bucket from which she sprinkled corn. She had new white boots that flashed red lights as she walked. "Corn, corn, corn," she sang along with Bill, a strange bleating utterance that resembled the sounds the deer make in crowded situations.

Two-year-old Cassandra, too small to manage the snow on her own, stood inside the front door and squealed each time she saw another deer appear, a high-pitched screech of joy. I could count the deer by counting her cries – 18, 19, 20, 21. Behind Amber and Bill came the deer. A river of deer surrounded the house. It was beautiful.

We fed the deer for three more years before we stopped. Some deer, however, still seem to remember our earlier generosity; five years later they edge close to the window and peer inside, accusing me with their eyes, reminding me that we'd once promised them food if they came to dine.

Eating Their Way
through Winter

Every winter, I keep our feeders filled with black-oil sunflower seeds and stuff suet baskets with a homemade concoction of suet, peanut butter, cornmeal, nuts and berries for the chickadees and nuthatches that remain behind to winter on the lakeshore.

One winter, after a howling snowstorm and sudden precipitous dip in temperature, my chickadees disappeared. Before the storm, several dozen chickadees were politely waiting their turn at the feeder, popping on and off the nearby Juneberry tree to grab a sunflower seed before flitting back to the tree to dine. The next day they were gone. Instead of chickadees, my feeders were swarming with redpolls, a bird with which I'd had little acquaintance until then. Though I found the redpolls' plump little bodies, red crowns and blushing breasts enchanting, I sorely missed the chickadees. Several times a day for over three weeks, I checked the feeders, hoping for a glimpse of those jaunty little black caps. During that time I saw only one chickadee. Then it, too, disappeared.

The *Birder's Handbook* states that chickadees – unlike redpolls that possess esophageal diverticulums (throat pockets where they store seeds that carry them through especially bad weather) – must eat continuously during winter's short daylight hours to gain 10 percent of their body weight in fat. Chickadees must "stoke their metabolic fires," or they will die. This compares to a 150-pound person gaining 15 pounds by nightfall and burning it off by morning. Sounds like eaters' heaven, doesn't it, save that it requires so much work to find and burn that food. Shivering all night, as do the chickadees, seems a miserable way to lose weight.

I found the chickadees eventually, not at my home but up the road a bit, where hundreds of them flitted about, darting to the feeder, climbing, dangling and dashing in and out of spruce trees with their thick clumps of needles to shelter and protect those tiny denizens of winter land.

We had no spruce or evergreens around our feeders. What we had, instead, was an unobstructed view of the Lake. I'm not sure if our home's former owner wanted a clear view of Lake Superior, or if there were no evergreens to begin with; nevertheless, the view of the Lake was what had drawn us to this particular piece of property. Our property was once, back in the late 19th and early 20th century, part of the John Schroeder Lumber Company campground that had housed more than 1,000 lumberjacks. They'd not only denuded the area of its forests of old-growth white pine, but also stripped the shoreline of its trees to make room for the campsite.

Although we've planted more than 200 baby spruce trees on our property, we hadn't thought of planting spruce near the shore where the bird feeders hang. Instead, we'd planted mountain ash on the lakeside thinking they would attract berry-loving birds. Unfortunately, deer love mountain ash, too. They demolished the seedlings before they'd had a chance to bloom.

Three years ago, Bill and I planted six good-sized spruce trees near our bird feeders to provide shelter for wintering birds. When full grown, they will probably interrupt our unobstructed view of the Lake. Though now only three to four feet in height, these spruce have already made a difference in the number of chickadees that hang around our house all winter. In spring and fall, those same young spruce trees host myriad migrating warblers on their way north. Not a bad exchange when a view of the Lake includes hundreds of jaunty chickadees and brightly colored warblers.

Jubilance in Gray

When gray-draped days in winter outnumber those wearing sunshine, I've been amazed to discover the variety and density of tones in which gray can show itself.

Take for instance the menacing leaden gray of clouds that some North Shore winter mornings feature. When those darkening clouds appear, Lake Superior dons a mantle of burnished pewter, and a palette of violet-gray hues texture the moisture-laden air. Even our driveway wears different shades of gray – the unbleached wool of roadside slush and the red-gray muck of tire tracks. Copper-colored in summer, the deer wear taupe-gray coats in winter, and snow, pristine white when it falls, gradually assumes a stippled gray veil from wind-blown dust and ash.

Every splash of bright color on such days – the reds of the wild mountain-ash berries, the ochre and gold fans of the willows – is cause for celebration. On one particularly ultra-gray late winter morning, I left the house just as dawn breached the night and heard the wondrous whispery buzz of a large flock of cedar waxwings in migration, stopping to dine on our mountain ash berries.

It was easy to locate the flock as the green-gray birds fluttered in and out of the high branches of nearby aspen and spruce on their way to the mountain ash. Periodically, a small flurry would lift and fly away from the ash trees, presumably having finished dining, making room for the next batch of waxwings that flew in to take their places. The ruby pith of the berries speckled the snow like paint flicked onto rice paper.

The waxwings soared upward and sank again like a gossamer shawl shaken in the wind, whispering their high-pitched insistent calls. I watched for close to 10 minutes before the birds lifted in a mini-vortex and flew directly above me. When I resumed walking, taking the path downhill toward the Lake to follow the shoreline, the birds accompanied me. They swirled in front of and behind me in total silence. No whispery buzzing to tell me they were there. When they rose high, they looked like small arrows with sharply pointed tips; when they dipped toward me, they resembled paper airplanes.

As I walked, accompanied by the silent waxwings, I heard other birdsong. Some of the calls were so melodious that I was certain I'd never heard them before. They were clear and penetrating and liquid but brief, as if the songster was not sure of its timing, not quite certain whether this surprising warmth meant that spring had arrived. I remember that morning as filled with color, not as color seen … but of color sensed and experienced. I returned home exhilarated and excited, buoyant, even jubilant – words not usually associated with an ongoing series of gray and overcast days but words that best describe the color of joy.

Minute by Minute

In late March 2006, I returned home exhausted. I'd just spent five hectic days in New York City, wending my way past piles of garbage (uncollected because 26 inches of snow had blocked the city curbs a day earlier) along streets packed with rushing pedestrians and honking taxis and belching buses to meetings with the New York press that was publishing my first book.

Throughout the flight and long drive back, our home beckoned like a Shangri-La, offering the promise of quietude and peace. As I turned down our driveway, the Lake immediately fulfilled its promise. I felt the tension slip from my shoulders like a heavy cloak and was able to breathe more deeply. I went to bed that night, expecting to awake the next morning in a similar relaxed state. Instead I discovered that rather than leaving New York, I'd brought New York home with me.

"What is the good of having silence throughout the neighborhood if one's emotions are in turmoil?" wrote the Roman Stoic philosopher Seneca, penning this statement from his lodgings above a public bathhouse where people leaped noisily into pools, masseuses pummeled shoulders, weightlifters grunted and hair removers tormented their clients "by plucking ... armpits."

My home is no noisy bathhouse, but my mind that morning bore a close resemblance to that unfortunate habitation. Despite the vast, soul-expanding view of the Lake and the quiet of my early morning rituals, thoughts tumbled with me from bed with as much energy as children leaping onto trampolines. Trying to quiet these rambunctious playmates felt like diving under water into momentary silence only to re-emerge into the pull and crash of wild surf.

It was obvious that finding the perfect place to live a deeper, more meaningful life – that silent neighborhood of which Seneca wrote – didn't guarantee the attainment of that goal. Instead my mind roiled with all the busy things I needed to do to catch up from my week away. Unpack, do the laundry, water the plants, get the mail, finish the article, answer requests, create a website, write a blog, pay the bills, make phone calls, answer letters. Meanwhile, right outside my window, Lake Superior lay serene and quiet, as reflective as I was not.

"So, your mind is a mess," I told myself. "Accept it! So you can't meditate. Accept it. Just be here. Now. For this minute." I wonder why it is that we rush around berating ourselves or trying to make time for what's important when we've got this minute in which to slow down? I remember having overheard a young man counsel his even younger co-worker. "You work real good slow," he'd said. They were leaning on their rakes in a city park, taking a break from their landscaping activities.

I'd had surgery on my right hand a day earlier and would be heading home that afternoon to try to make do with only one hand. Doing even the smallest things took inordinate amounts of time. I thought of that young man's remark often as I struggled to prepare food with one hand; to get dressed with one hand; to use the computer with one hand. He saw that his companion did a much better job while working slowly. "Attentively" is probably the best word to describe that way of working.

"Sometimes the most important thing in a whole day is the rest we take between two deep breaths, or the turning inwards in prayer for five short minutes," wrote Ettie Hillesum, the young Jewish mystic whose diaries, written between the years 1941 and 1943 (when she died at Auschwitz), have inspired millions.

To take that rest "between two deep breaths" is to open ourselves to astonishment, to reverence and gratitude. The ancient monks knew this and constructed their way of life accordingly. In our modern-day haste to accomplish great things, we forget that its the journey that matters, not the destination. Considering that our final destination is death, do we really want to rush through our days to get there?

"Today is the only guarantee you get," writes Anna Quindlen in *A Short Guide to a Happy Life*. She tells of interviewing a homeless man on the boardwalk at Coney Island and asking him why he didn't go to one of the shelters.

"Look at the view, young lady. Look at the view," he'd responded. The Lake repeats this message whenever I am tempted to busy myself with worthless worries and mindless to-dos.

Does Lake Superior Freeze?

No matter how often one visits the North Shore in winter, it is rare to find Lake Superior completely covered with ice.

The coming and going of lake ice is a common experience for those of us newcomers who live on the shore. We know little else. A number of Schroeder old-timers, however, have memories of the Lake frozen solid every winter. They skated on its surface. They said that skating the 34 miles from Schroeder to Grand Marais was not impossible back then, though none ever claimed having done so.

I walked on Lake Superior once – one of a large group that gathered at the Sugarloaf Interpretive Center in Schroeder to hear environmental educator Andrew Slade speak about the Lake Superior ice phenomenon. Slade described the Lake as acting like a thermal flywheel: a large object that takes a long time to move, moderating by its inertia any fluctuation of speed. That is why, though January and February flaunted ongoing days of subzero temperatures, the ice did not form until March. Satellite images taken that day, March 12, 2003, showed Lake Superior completely frozen. Slade didn't buy it. He quipped that unless one could drive across the Lake from Minnesota to Michigan, the Lake wasn't completely frozen. Nonetheless, we followed Slade onto Lake Superior that morning, clambering over walls of ice to walk "on water" across a frozen Lake Superior from the Sugarloaf beach to the Sugarloaf peninsula.

According to an article posted in the climate section of the University of Minnesota's website, Lake Superior was only 90 percent frozen over in 2003 when we followed Slade onto the ice.

Records from the Great Lakes Aquarium in Duluth show that the most recent complete covers of Lake Superior happened in 1962, 1979 and 1996, when the former owner of our home watched a pack of wolves down a deer on its surface. Covered solid or not, Lake Superior provides some spectacular ice events.

A blizzard in March 2007 spewed ice boulders, some the size of tabletops, 30 feet into the air. The thunderous roar of what sounded like squadrons of bombers kept us awake all night. Unable to sleep because of the noise, we watched in amazement as immense iron-gray waves laden with glacial armor hurled themselves against the hills they'd begun building the day before, turning them into mountains. Along the shoreline, as far as we could see, geysers plumed skyward every fifth or seventh wave, building those masses ever higher. When the blizzard finally cleared, Bill and I donned snowshoes and hiked along the shore to Taconite Harbor, where an Everest of ice dwarfed everything we'd seen till then. Bill estimated it could have been 70 feet high. Despite that storm and the size of those ice mountains, the Lake never froze completely in 2007.

Bill and I were not here during the bitter winter of 2009, when NOAA satellite shots show the Lake covered with ice. We were in Florida, enduring the noise, the crowds and the craziness. This winter we've seen no ice at all, and NOAA shots show the Lake almost completely ice-free – a scary scenario when ice prevents the massive water evaporation that occurs in winter because the air is so dry. Because we had so little snow and ice cover this winter, we moved into spring with some of the worst drought conditions ever monitored up here. I thought I might be seeing a lot more of my Nessie's back this year. Heavy rains, however, have alleviated most of the danger, and the water rushing down our rivers into the Lake is doing a good job in turning my monster rock almost invisible.

Seasons
of Learning
Spring

A Cherry
Walking Stick

After spending a very wet weekend with us, my cousin Paul made me a beautiful hand-carved walking stick from a piece of cherry wood. He made it knowing that water on the North Shore means mud on the trails and walking sticks provide good support in slippery situations. He forgot the one problem generated by hand-carved walking sticks. When beloved cousins make them, they attain status as objets d'art rather than as useful tools.

Paul was my hero when I was a child. He was handsome, blond and five years older than I was. Paul often spent summers at our home, where he and my brother Steve became inseparable companions. I remember them ricocheting off the diving board into the icy waters of the lake by our home, splashing one another with oars from the old wooden rowboat, the stench emanating from the immense snapping turtle they'd killed and hung to dry, wanting the shell but neglecting to remove the flesh.

With such memories attached to its maker, the cherry walking stick remained unused – propped next to the front door for all to admire. Meanwhile, I continued to hike as I always had, without props. That is, I hiked this way until a certain early thaw turned one hike into a mishap. I rose from a brief rest on a lovely rock and took off, like a rocket, downhill on my backside. Since then, the cherry walking stick has come with me on every hike I take, wet weather or not. It not only breaks falls, but it makes a great pitching tool for lofting fallen branches off the trail.

As I stride purposefully and securely along the trail, blessing Paul's foresight, an image comes to mind of the elderly German couple who surged past Bill and me as we struggled up the side of a glacier toward the Harding Ice Field in Alaska. They looked so jaunty with their little feathered hiking caps, their high woolen socks and suede shorts and alpine walking sticks. Several hours later they passed us again, this time coming from the opposite direction. Had they made it to the top, I asked, doubting that they had gotten there and back again while we were still miles from our goal. "Of course," the woman said snorting derisively. "It's an easy trail." Her husband smiled timidly, and then hurried after his wife who, walking stick beating tempo, had already disappeared around a pile of shale.

On Board
an Ore Boat

At night the ore boats glide past our picture windows –
transformed into floating palaces with winking lights. By day they
plow furrows in the great prairie of the Lake. Sightings like these
helped reconcile us to our home's proximity to Taconite Harbor
with all its thrumming noise and belching smoke. Because the
harbor is sometimes the ore boats' destination, we get to see those
boats better than most North Shore residents do. Unlike most
North Shore residents, I've been aboard an ore boat as a guest.

When Marion C., a fellow historical society member, drove to
fetch her mail at the Schroeder post office on a Tuesday in early
April 1999, she overheard Ken Michaels, first mate of the *Kaye E.
Barker*, an ore boat then docked at Taconite Harbor, asking if
Schroeder had a notary public. Schroeder did not have a notary,
but Tofte, three miles up the highway, did. Marion offered to drive
Michaels there. He in turn invited Marion to tour his ore boat.
"Bring some friends," he suggested, and she did.

At three o'clock that afternoon Marion, Lavonne A. and I
drove down to the dock where the *Kaye E. Barker*, Cleveland,
emptied of cargo and waiting for a load of taconite, sat high in the
water. I saw a ladder teetering against the gangplank high overhead
and realized we'd have to climb it. I almost changed my mind
about touring the ore boat, but knew that I'd never forgive
myself if I turned tail. Pretending nonchalance, I climbed the
ladder carefully and gratefully seized the hand a seaman offered
when I reached the top. "Now, that wasn't so bad was it?" he asked,
smiling.

"It wasn't bad at all," I responded, embarrassed that he'd detected the quaver in my voice when I'd thanked him.

The expression "shipshape" meant exactly that on the *Kaye E. Barker*. The floors gleamed beneath our feet. The engine room we toured was being painted white. White, mind you! I remembered clearing a greasy, soot-laden furnace room when I was a young nun and couldn't imagine painting that place white. Even deep in the ship's bowels, among the belts from which coal had been unloaded and into which taconite pellets would soon descend, the decks were freshly hosed and clean.

It was only 4 p.m. when our tour guide Don Donovan announced dinner. A smorgasbord of salads, swordfish, lamb chops, fried chicken, parsley potatoes, wild rice and rotini pasta awaited us. For dessert, a choice of fresh chocolate cake, lemon bars, ice cream and thin slivers of the creamiest fudge ever concocted.

While the crew members made themselves scarce on our arrival, Pete, the salad and pastry chef, hovered about, refilling our glasses with iced tea as we chatted with Captain Albert Tielke and Second Mate Tim Dawson. The captain accompanied us when we toured the bridge. From the windows of the comfortably furnished guest quarters, we watched thick gray waterfalls of taconite pellets cascading into each of the ship's holds. Once the bins filled, we would have to depart quickly as the boat would immediately leave port. In farewell, Donovan plied us with ship-baked cookies and fresh grapes, then hurried us along the immense deck toward the gangplank. How would we negotiate the steep climb down with all this bounty, I wondered. Weighted with taconite pellets, however, the *Kaye E. Barker* sat low enough to allow easy access from gangplank to dock. A crewman was there to assist us as we stepped down. Every mother should be so treated!

As soon as we'd disembarked, the gangplank was raised and with several ear-shattering blasts of her horn the *Kaye E. Barker* signaled its departure. She moved from the harbor midst a swirling, screaming flock of sea gulls that rose in protest around her. When I arrived home 10 minutes later, she was gliding past our house. I waved wildly and felt the warmth of our visit extend across the Lake. I watched until she was out of sight.

With the sale of Taconite Harbor to Minnesota Power, we don't see the ore boats nearly as often. Only when a new shipment of coal is being delivered do we hear the blast of a horn announcing the presence of an ore boat in our neighborhood. I welcome the sound.

Eating the Trees

In early May 1999, the Minnesota Department of Transportation began extensive expansion of Highway 61 through our Schroeder neighborhood. Excavators and backhoes arrived to rip up the old highway and clear the easements to make room for widening. Those machines reminded me of huge yellow dinosaurs as they dropped their heavy heads and swiped their teeth across the terrain, uprooting spruce and birch with each mouthful. The snapping of roots and branches accompanied the drone of their growls and beeps. In little over three hours, they'd devoured both sides of the highway, stacking the bones of their meal in immense and twisted heaps for burning.

Although Highway 61 was too narrow to handle the growing traffic congestion along the North Shore, it was painful to watch its widening. When it came to our beautiful old spruce trees being uprooted to make room, my feelings grew protective. There were already too few large old pines in this section of the North Shore where dying birch predominated. The Schroeder children took action, focusing on a cluster of beautiful red pines and cedars near the wayside, and posting notes wrapped with duct tape around those trees. "Don't cut me down." "Please let me grow." "Help save us." "Don't hurt me, I'm your friend. I help you breathe." "Please leave as many trees as possible. We want them here in Schroeder as long as we live." A fifth-grader, Dan Mensen, even faxed a message to an official at the highway department, asking him to help try to save those trees. I doubt even a miracle worker could have widened the highway and saved those trees. Several large evergreens did survive the holocaust, however: The one red pine and two white spruce in front of Bob Silver's property.

Bill managed to save 120 small white spruce seedlings from demolition by digging them up before the backhoes destroyed them. On the weekend that Bill worked to rescue and replant those seedlings along our driveway, I headed up to the Temperance River State Park on a similar project: the transplanting of 1,000 white pine seedlings along the park's lakeshore. The bulk of the work involved cutting fencing into 10-by-6-foot sections, clipping these sections into rings and moving the resulting cages to the planting site. Cars, trucks, and vans filled the parking area and roadside. Children of all sizes milled about (except for the one still in the back carrier) as adults confronted multiple bales of uncut wire. I was responsible for carrying the completed cages and support bars down the hill and into the woods where blue flags identified newly planted pines. Those cages would protect the seedlings until they were tall enough for the top terminal bud to be out of reach of foraging deer. As the project had only enough money for 550 cages, we placed the cages over alternate seedlings, selecting those that looked the sturdiest and most likely to survive.

An 8-year-old Cub Scout from the Gunflint Trail assisted me. While other Scouts helped make cages or gathered up the tires, pop bottles, cans and other detritus hidden in woods, Luke scouted the seedlings, plotted our path and held back brambles and branches so I could get through with the cages. Before long we were sweating despite the 40-degree temperature. The cages beat bruises into my hips. Luke tripped and tore his pants. We tied a fluorescent pink ribbon on each cage and then sallied forth in search of more seedlings.

Of the 120 seedlings Bill replanted that weekend, only 30 or so survived despite our efforts to protect, feed and water them. Those that made it have grown in relation to the amount of sun they've gotten. Some are now 4 feet tall while others remain only 2 to 3 feet tall. We keep planting trees – mountain ash for the birds who love the berries, white and red pines and spruce trees to take the place of the birch and aspen trees that seem bent on dying from the tops down. Unless they threaten to fall on our home, we leave the dead trees standing. Visitors sometimes ask why we don't clean them up, not understanding that to do so would be to destroy an entire environmental economy supporting forest renewal and the wild creatures small and large that depend on those dead trees for sustenance and for homes.

Tree planting efforts take place every spring throughout Minnesota's Arrowhead region to restore the white pine that were logged out when the area was opened to settlement. The effort to replenish aging second-growth forests with spruce and cedar, and to replant areas destroyed by fire, continues to take place along the shore and throughout the Arrowhead – a communal effort to cherish and nurture the land that supports us.

Swinging in Schroeder

While highway reconstruction was taking place at the head of our driveway, Bob Silver, who would celebrate his 86th birthday that June, was erecting the wondrous cedar swing we'd commissioned him to build for us. Bob clambered on top of its supporting beam like a much younger man to mark plumb with the horizon rather than with an instrument. Below him, neighbor Bruce Martinson and Bill helped with picks, jacks and wrenches to stabilize and fasten the swing. Several hours later, the four of us fit comfortably in that swing. We leaned back, lifted our feet from the earth and glided toward the Lake and back again. Bob, who'd already tested the swing in his workshop, claimed that one push could generate more than 20 glides.

Bill and I spent much of Mother's Day testing it. With the sun warm and the birch trees budding, we swung in the dappled light, indulging ourselves for hours. That night we returned to our swing and rocked while gazing at the stars and listening to the Lake gurgle around Nessie and along our lakeshore.

The arrival of our cedar swing triggered a full-blown case of spring fever. The symptoms had been building for weeks. Any excuse was sufficient to leave the home office and escape for the day. The white spruce seedlings needed watering, the garden required weeding and the bird feeders had to be cleaned and refilled. Other friends suffered from the same ailment. They called to tempt me away from the computer for a hike in the woods in search of birds or a drive up the back roads on a jaunt in pursuit of wildflowers.

That spring, my first on the North Shore, opened my eyes to all the small gifts hidden in the present moment – the flash of white along the trail that might be bloodroot or spring violets, the mysterious trill of the winter wren, the spicy sweetness of the trailing arbutus. Nature sequesters gems throughout this land and one must slow down to find them. Spring fever practically guarantees our slowing down, and our cedar swing picks up the slack. Like a fisherman in his boat on a tranquil lake, like a mother and babe in a rocking chair, I can put the world to rest from our swing. From within the arc of its embrace I can open myself to all this place has to share. Bob said that our swing should last for more than 40 years. That should yield enough fully conscious moments to feed a lifetime.

Graves for the
Living

We'd lived in Schroeder for 10 months when Bill and I purchased a family grave in Schroeder's tiny hillside cemetery. We thought it a lovely spot from which to await resurrection, with its view of the Lake, the shade of the big spruce trees and a lavender phlox blanket creeping across the grass. It wasn't the purchase price (then $4 a plot for residents) that inspired our buy, but the determination to make this our home 'till death do us part.

The owning of a few acres of land on the North Shore has given me something that my other homes lacked, a sense of belonging. My other homes, though lovely, were tucked into wee bits of space, with barely enough land to hold the house together. I could not picture myself spending the rest of my life in any of those houses. Even as a child, as we moved from one lovely place to another – a lakeside home in Saddle River, New Jersey, to an oceanfront condominium in San Juan, Puerto Rico – I'd felt adrift. My parents must have felt this too because they never bought a family plot. My father lies buried in Puerto Rico, sharing a grave with a doctor he never met. My mother lies in New Jersey, buried in the same plot as my first husband, Vittorio.

Bill's family, on the other hand, believes in family plots. Most of them have continued to live and to die in the place they've called home for generations. The acres of land they have farmed in Iowa hold them together. Some of their tombstones bear engravings of these farms, the houses, barns and surrounding landscape all lovingly detailed. One could drive around the countryside and identify family farms by the landscapes on their tombstones. What impressed me about these tombstones and family plots was the foresight they reflected. They were monuments for the living, the names of their future residents clearly marked and birth dates noted, while date of death remained conspicuously empty. I attributed this preparedness to their German heritage and to what I thought of as a farmer's familiarity with death.

From a perspective changed by six acres of paradise, I now think I know why Iowans take their farms to their burial sites. It is the land. They love it just as I have grown to love this land. Like Bill's family, I have purchased a family plot in the place where I've set down roots. This is my home and I hope to remain here, in one form or another, forever.

Birds, Binoculars and Festivals

From childhood on, I've enjoyed watching birds and listening to their songs, but our move to the North Shore inspired me to do more than watch and listen. It convinced me that I ought to learn to identify the birds that live here.

I began my bird learning lessons by buying Peterson's *Birding by Ear* tapes and several different birding field guides. I also bought a pair of binoculars so that I could spot the songster while it was singing. After a few weeks of diligent tape listening and binocular viewing, I came to the conclusion that I was both aurally limited and binocularly challenged.

A Boreal Birding Festival slated for June 1999 offered a firsthand opportunity to connect bird songs with bird shapes and to give them names. We'd be bird watching with experts. The only difficulty lay in the distance between our home and the festival, which was on the Gunflint Trail, 75.3 miles away. The distance issue was resolved when our good friends Frank and Mary Alice Hansen invited us to share their camper that weekend.

Bill and I thought we'd make a full weekend of the event, so even though the festival would not begin until that evening, we planned to spend the day in Grand Marais, dine with the Hansens that evening in town and then drive with them to the festival. Those were the plans until Bill's eye made contact with a very pointy stick.

Bill had faithfully worn his safety glasses all week as he sawed fallen trees and mowed the rocks in our lawn, but he wasn't wearing them when he stooped to pick up some loose brush in the driveway just before leaving. Instead of spending Friday afternoon enjoying Grand Marais as we had planned, we sat in the Sawtooth Clinic while the doctor treated Bill's eye.

Bill's eye cleansed and sedated, he said he felt well enough to join Frank and Mary Alice for supper and continue on to the festival. Anxious to attend the festival, I didn't insist we return home as another good wife might have done. The pain meds worked through supper with the Hansens, but by the time we arrived at the festival, Bill's eye had changed its mind. It didn't want to be there.

Bill once again disagreed. He might as well suffer at the festival as at home, he said. And once again I gratefully accepted his determination. By the time the festival started, Bill's eye was giving him so much trouble that field trips were out of the question. Frank, bless him, offered to stay with Bill while Mary Alice and I went birding.

As it turned out, I could have left my binoculars at home. The Northern Waterthrush taunted even the experts by singing without stop while remaining invisible, as did the least flycatcher, the hermit thrush and black-throated blue warbler. When a three-toed woodpecker was actually spotted, everyone swung their binoculars in that direction. "Where?" I queried. "There," they said. "You can't miss it." Well, maybe they couldn't, but I could. I swung my binoculars in the direction they pointed, but captured only leaves and tree branches in the binocular lenses. I was comforted to notice that one woman – local birding expert Molly Hoffman – remained unperturbed. Indeed she rarely lifted her binoculars and seemed to take greater pleasure in identifying the birds by their songs than in seeing them.

"Do you hear that? Zzzzzzeeeurp. Northern parula." She cocked her head and murmured. "Sleetsleetsleetsleetsleeteeseeee. Blackburnian warbler." During this event I learned seven new birdsongs without even needing my eyes.

Whether or not black flies can see, they made it clear that I had worn the wrong colors to the Gunflint. The flies ignored those wearing beige and mobbed those in blue. I suffered their bites as reparation for not having insisted on taking Bill home Friday night. While Bill spent a weekend in misery, even the weeping black fly bites that adorned my neck and ankles failed to dampen my enthusiasm.

My difficulties with binoculars, however, continued to plague me. Determined to succeed, I began practicing at home, sitting at my dining room window, selecting a particular branch on the Juneberry tree and putting the lenses to my eyes. My focus was usually several feet off the mark, somewhere in the Lake or on a nearby shrub. I'd try again, concentrating on the branch while slowly raising the binoculars. While I might have missed the branch, I sometimes accidentally found a bird. Once, in this manner, I discovered a tree filled with migrating warblers.

A pileated woodpecker should be easy to see. It's so big. So bright. I was on another of my many Superior Hiking Trail excursions when I spotted the bright red topknot of the pileated as it gorged on something high up on a dying birch. I inched my binoculars upward to get a good close-up look at that large bird and discovered instead a maple in bud. A beautiful sight, but not the one I wanted. I lowered the binoculars, fastened my eyes on the red topknot once more and raised the binoculars. The soft gray striations of bark emerged, but no woodpecker. When I finally had the woodpecker within my sights, I kept the binoculars glued to my face, afraid to lose focus. My neck started to ache. My arms trembled. I lowered the binoculars, hoping I'd conquered the art. Just for luck, I tried again … and failed.

Later, while hiking back to the trailhead, I was startled by a wild kuk-kuk-keekeekeekee and looked up in time to see the pileated woodpecker launch from the maple to which he'd been clinging and soar through the naked trees like an ecstatic teen with a bright red mohawk.

I am happy to report that with 12 years of practice, I have become a fairly adept user of binoculars. I can sit at my dining room window and zero in on the goldeneye swimming a good 200 feet out on the Lake. I've grown well acquainted with the bad-hair days of the red-breasted merganser and even managed to follow a yellow-rumped warbler as it hopped from branch to branch in a Juneberry tree.

I still have difficulty, however, finding where in the woods that bird is singing, with or without binoculars.

Sightings

The young moose eyed us warily. Bill and I stood transfixed, unable to believe that we'd really encountered a moose this close to home. When we'd left the house early that morning, I'd joked that maybe this would be the day we'd meet a moose. We'd both laughed because we'd been looking for moose ever since we'd moved here. I'd even dragged Bill out of bed before dawn to drive forestry roads to look for moose, sitting in the car for hours as the morning mist rose from swampy land that I thought looked like prime moose territory. We'd once spent half an hour watching the roots of a dead tree in a swamp because my sister-in-law was convinced they were a moose's antlers. I was convinced that if we were diligent about these searches, we would find what we were looking for. I was like the woman who, having seen a moose crossing sign, asked our local postmaster what time the moose crossed.

Animal sightings, I've since learned, come when you least expect them, as with the young moose we'd encountered on the Tote Road. Even more surprising was the morning we unknowingly approached within 50 feet of a moose dining on water lilies in Boneye's Meadow. If I were a moose, that's where I'd hang out, I'd often told Bill, but until that morning all we'd ever seen in that swamp were red-winged blackbirds, tall reeds and cattails. Bill saw him first, spotting him through the cedar trees that separated the trail from the swamp. He motioned for me to move slowly. I did.

Bill and I certainly never expected to set out to hike and meet moose, nor did we ever expect to encounter, on foot, a bear crossing our driveway as we set out on another dawn hike. We were as surprised as the bear was. We stopped. The bear stopped. He stood there eyeing us for a few seconds, then finding us of little interest, continued across the driveway and into the woods. Neither Bill nor I had a chance to experience fear, so fast was that encounter.

Long before we ever came upon an animal in the wild, however, we'd found their signs. We'd squished through mud where moose, preceding us on the trail, had left the huge imprints of their hooves for us to thrill over. We found moose dung equally amazing – perfect ovals the size of very large beads.

I was a very new newcomer; the first time, I almost stepped on wolf scat deposit in the middle of a trail. At the time, I didn't know whether the hair-and-bone-filled droppings had been left by a large dog, a wolf or a bear. Did bears eat hairy things? Did dogs? What did bear droppings look like anyway? I had more questions than a 3-year-old.

Less common, but just as puzzling, was encountering an animal in the wild and not knowing what the heck it was, as happened to us while hiking the Brule River section of the Superior Hiking Trail. Contrary to our usual hiking mode, I was in the lead when a sudden movement on a nearby aspen caught my attention. With the sun behind it, the shadowy back-lit animal clinging to the narrow trunk looked like a monkey. I stopped so as not to frighten the creature, which, perhaps reassured by my lack of aggression, unfolded, revealing a lavish chocolate tail and glistening fur. Thinking I'd seen a pine marten, I alerted Bill, whereupon the animal leaped onto another tree and disappeared.

Bill insisted the animal's ears were rounded, whereas I thought they looked downright fox-like. My uncertainty about the pine marten's identity increased as I recalled its languid unfolding, more like the unrolling of a swath of mahogany-colored velvet than the "luxuriantly furred lightning bolt of the forest" that I'd read about. In a woods too shaded to clearly detect such markings, neither Bill nor I had seen the pale orange throat patch that might have cinched the pine marten's identification.

Our collection of books on flowers, birds, hiking and skiing trails and local history expanded to include a few books on animals. *Peterson's Animal Tracks* answered most of my scat and track questions. It featured sketches of both tracks and scat with scaled measurements for both, including the shape, color and contents of the scat. The hairy, toothy droppings we found on the Superior Hiking Trail were those of a wolf. The berry-filled, sometimes hairy, dung on our driveway belonged to a bear and so on.

While I am now much more fluent in the language of animal sightings, I remain impatient with my ignorance. I have to remind myself that intimacy is acquired slowly, that place reveals itself one day at a time and that in the end it is not the accumulation of facts that matter but the wisdom born of the journey.

Persistence
Is the Key

There's an attribute that separates a real fan of nature from a dilettante. Its name? Persistence. I learned about this quality one May evening in 1999 when I found myself lying on my back in a rocky, stubble-filled field, swatting gnats, black flies and mosquitoes while waiting for dusk. Dory Spence, the bird lover who lured me into that field, had already spent many spring evenings in this manner. Doing what? Why, waiting for woodcocks to mate, of course.

Dory lives around a mile from our home. We met for the first time while helping to transplant white pines at the Temperance River State Park. When she learned that I was interested in birds, she asked if I'd like to join her one evening to see the woodcocks perform their amazing mating ritual.

"And then it was evening … and the American woodcocks, those odd snipes of the boggy woods, were performing their courtship song-flights on all sides of us. We could hear four or five of them at once. Their nasal beeping call notes from the ground would give way to a twittering, bubbling song in the air, and occasionally we would see the chunky silhouette of a woodcock in flight against the darkening sky."

I share this lovely snippet from Ken Kaufmann's *Kingbird Highway* to help you understand why bird lovers would lie in bug-infested meadows waiting to see the woodcock court a mate. The night I joined Dory, the woodcocks avoided the field in which we lay, but the gnats and mosquitoes were there in droves. While I usually stay as far from buggy places as I can, insects do not deter

Dory. She continues to share her evenings with them, awaiting the arrival of the little suitors.

The late Virginia Burandt, my elderly quilting friend, was another persistent North Shore nature watcher, a wild flower devotee who introduced me to the county's back roads and logging trails. "There's a whole world up there," she'd urged.

On our first jaunt into the back country, Virginia joyfully pointed out tire marks that zigzagged across the gravel roadway. "See those?" she sang. "They are my tracks. I must have seen something there." Sure enough, "there" we'd find some wondrous flower, like the trout lily hidden to all but the most discerning eyes. One set of tire tracks actually careened off the road into a ditch. Virginia giggled when she saw them. "Oh, how I'd love to be able to claim those as my own but they are unfortunately not mine. Someone like me, I think."

I told Virginia that I'd seen a showy lady's slipper growing near a bog. "Oh!" she exclaimed with excitement. "There's an entire hillside covered with yellow lady's slippers in Grand Portage. Let's go find them!" She was certain she could remember the exact hillside, and if she was correct, they should be blooming now. So off we went in search of the yellow lady's slippers which Virginia claimed we'd see on Highway 17 in Grand Portage. As we crawled along Highway 17 seeking the elusive flower Virginia kept claiming, "This is not it. I don't recognize this road at all."

"But it has to be," I sighed. "The sign said 17." Disheartened by our lack of success, we stopped for lunch at Grand Portage Lodge where Virginia immediately began to query everyone she met. How does one explain that Highway 17 is not the Highway 17 one remembers and still sound sane? People were kind but vague. They couldn't help us.

I would have called the search quits at this point, but Virginia was not ready to give up. We made one final effort to locate the road before heading home. At the Grand Portage Forestry Center, we found a small map showing that the "Old Highway 61" (which we'd bypassed) was actually the elusive Highway 17. And on that road, right where she said they'd be, a whole hillside of blooming yellow lady's slippers danced for us in the breeze.

Virginia and Dory taught me a lot about persistence. I learned that if I'm to become more than just a nature dilettante, I must work more diligently to cultivate persistence as a virtue.

A Name of
Your Own

From the top of the ridge where I'd stopped to rest, I could see Lake Superior. It was early May and the Lake wore serene blue. Between the Lake and the ridge stretched an undulating swath of woods that dipped into sudden valleys and then climbed the jagged edge of the Sawtooth Mountains. I made room for myself among the greening grasses and let my eyes rove over the landscape. The silvery and mauve hues of aspen and birch catkins dominated the valley below, punctuated by the dark spears of spruce, the lace of the cedar trees and luminous with the sudden reds of budding maples. From where I sat, some branches looked like they'd caught a sunset's brilliance; but it wasn't sunset, it was noon.

Beginning in early April, I'd hiked the same section of the Superior Hiking Trail – east toward the Temperance River from the Cramer Road trailhead. It was not a long hike, three miles at most, but rather than getting tedious and repetitive, this walk had become the highlight of every day. I hiked the same section of trail because I'd encountered scalloped sage green leaves pushing up from under maple leaves and wondered what they were. Curious to see what those leaves heralded, I went back on a daily basis to see what they'd look like when they blossomed.

A few days later, while reading Larry Weber's *Backyard Almanac*, as I did every morning, I learned that I could give some plants I didn't recognize names that were easy to recall. This delighted me. When I discovered swaths of tiny flowers with delicate pink- and lavender-threaded petals, I called them peppermint cups. The plant with the parsley-looking leaves and flowers that looked like tiny white flies, I called parsley and flies. The scalloped, sage-green leaves tucked tightly around folded white blooms that launched my curiosity, I named dancers because their scalloped leaves reminded me of capes a ballet dancer might use. As the white blooms opened to the sun, revealing their bright centers, the dancers seemed to fan those leaves like tutus. While I now know they are called bloodroot, I shall always think of them as dancers.

As the days progressed, the bloodroot appeared from behind trees and tumbled in small groups from sunny hollows. Spring beauties capered alongside the trail for miles. Tiny purple, yellow and white violets appeared everywhere, and the first leaves of what I later learned were marsh marigolds began to sprout in a boggy section where they made the boardwalk look as lush as a conservatory.

I took notes, sketching what I saw, stopping often to look at tiny flowers and mosses with a jeweler's loupe. What marvels the loupe revealed. Tucked within even the most minuscule flower were tender veins, itsy-bitsy bugs, delicate shadings in lovely colors, spiky pollen and other wonders I could not see with the naked eye.

Tracking the development of these woodland plants, from the first small leaves to push through forest duff, to the tightly curled bud, to the open flower; naming them, sketching them and learning their real names imprinted these early spring perennials on my mind so clearly that I've never forgotten their names.

As the entire woods started to burgeon with spring blooms – Solomon seal, twisted-stalk, blue-bead lily, false lily of the valley, sessile-leaved bellwort and lord knows how many other flowers – it became more difficult to hang onto all of their names. I remembered them during the time of their blooming but the following spring had to resort to rechecking the wildflower guides.

I once commented that if I believed in reincarnation, I'd make a point of becoming a naturalist in my next life. Word must have gotten around because the director of the naturalist program at Wolf Ridge called one day and said that I could become a naturalist by simple observation. All I had to do was select a particular site in the out-of-doors and return to it frequently to note the changes, what she called a longitudinal study. I didn't even have to know the names of the fungi and ferns, the insects or animals, the rocks, grasses, flowers or trees that grew and lived there. All I needed to do was to note and observe changes.

"Keep a journal. Track dates, temperature and precipitation and make notes and drawings of what you see." Tracking these changes had an impressive name: Phenology.

I realized I'd been doing this since I first encountered the scalloped leaves of the bloodroot and returned day after day to see what they were. I'd taken my notebook. I'd sketched leaves and buds and flowers. I'd given them descriptive names and later looked them up so that next time I visited I'd recognize and name them properly. While I might not know the names of every spring ephemeral I've encountered in the woods, I know enough to sound like an expert when hiking with friends.

Knowing How
to Dress

I've been living on the North Shore for 12 years and I still don't know how to dress. I don't mean deciding whether to wear a skirt – my city-wear hit the discard pile right after we moved here. No. What I mean is how many layers do I wear today?

I'm a believer in layering. Though it is not a fool-proof method of dealing with the temperature, it is certainly better than arriving here in June bringing only sundresses and shorts, as my granddaughters have done. I have a favorite picture of Cassie, taken one summer when she was 3, draped in one of my sweatshirts and wearing my winter hat because she'd arrived without a single long sleeve shirt, sweater or jacket.

While the temperature can hover in the 80s Fahrenheit in Minneapolis, up here it can be 20, 30 or even 40 degrees colder. I once drove to the Cities and traveled through five different weather zones. Snow here, sun in Two Harbors, fog in Duluth, heat in Hinckley and rain in St. Paul.

I don't think I'm exaggerating when I say that the temperature on Lake Superior's shore can vary by 10 to 20 degrees a half mile inland or 500 feet up the hill. You can leave the house to hike the Superior Hiking Trail on a chill May morning when the temperature hovers in the low 40s, layered in silk undershirt, long-sleeved flannel shirt and wind-breaker, and discover that short sleeves, maybe even a tank top, would have been a better option.

In winter, snowshoeing and cross-country skiing can create such a sweat that you'll peel off everything down to your long underwear. You can always put it back on again, layer by layer, as you cool off.

It's spring that poses the difficulty. Stripping layer by layer might leave you in your long underwear, but where do you go from there? And if you chanced to discard some of those layers along the way (too hot to carry them), planning to retrieve them on the way back, that too can cause problems.

I was a still a hiking neophyte on the May morning I arrived at the Cramer Road trailhead dressed for the 40-degree weather as indicated by our outdoor thermometer. After hiking 15 minutes, I stripped off my jacket and tucked it, along with my mittens and hat, into the crevice of an old tree. Bathed in the lovely warmth of the May sun, I took my time, stopping often to examine growing things with my loupe or scanning the trees for the black-throated green warbler that seemed to be following me. Moseying along like this, poking into nature's wonders, I paid no attention to the clouds massing in the distance and was startled when the sun suddenly ducked behind a wall of black clouds and a harsh cold rode into the woods on the wind. The spruce began to sigh and the old maples and birch creaked.

I was high on an overlook when icy pellets of sleet slammed onto my head and shoulders. While I still had on my long underwear and a light wool sweater, I had little protection from the sleet and wind. My jacket, hat and mittens were well over a mile and a half away. Tucking my binoculars under my sweater, I ran as fast as a 60-something trekker can run, toward the cleft in the tree where I'd tucked my jacket, hat and mittens. Meanwhile, my friendly warbler deserted, leaving me to contend with the hail and the wind on my own. As the trees swayed and crackled above me, I wondered what would happen if I should be under one when it fell. I'd had to climb over too many fallen trees in the past to dismiss this possibility. How long would I lie there before another hiker came along? And what if lightning struck while I was under a tree while still up on the ridge? What if I met up with a galloping moose or a bear with cubs hurrying back to her den?

I thought of the merganser I'd watched that morning, contentedly bobbing and diving until a gull swooped down on it like a kamikaze fighter determined to kill. Repeatedly that white-winged fury dropped onto the merganser's head and each time the merganser dived, surfacing at a distance but not quite far enough away to avoid the next bombing. On the fifth dive, the merganser stayed under and the gull, after circling a few times, wheeled off.

Almost simultaneously the merganser popped up again. Safe. The memory lifted my spirits. I eventually made it back to my jacket, hat and mittens, and with their warmth comforting me, fear departed and hope returned. Like the merganser, I'd managed to elude the threat from above, but unlike that feathered fellow, I hadn't dressed for the weather.

Muskets and All

On our way to the Twin Cities to celebrate Easter 2001, Bill and I picked up three members of the Coalition of Historic Trekkers who were about to begin a re-enactment of an 18th century voyageur's journey. While the journey from Caribou Wayside to the Skou Road was far from the 1,200 miles Lake Superior voyageurs traversed, they were traveling in the same kind of clothing that the voyageurs wore, carried the same kinds of muskets and pots and bedrolls, and would eat the same kind of foods.

Karl Koster, a huge bear of a fellow and full-time 18th century re-enactor at the Grand Portage National Monument historic site, carried the iron pot that they'd use for cooking. Tom Burket, a former marketing person and stay-at-home dad, and Rick Seidemann, a social studies teacher, carried rucksacks packed with pemmican (fat with dried meat and sometimes dried berries), smoked sausage and fish, wild rice, dried peas and lentils, dried strawberries, seeds, beef soaked in vinegar and several loaves of home-baked bread. Woolen blankets, which they slung over their backs as bedrolls, and antique muskets and powder horns (which they'd carry but would not use), completed their camping equipment. No tents for these voyageurs. No gourmet-packaged meals. Just the joy of roughing it, as did their forefathers. Dressed only in woolen vests, long-sleeved linen shirts, wool britches, leather moccasins and leggings soaked in bear grease and tallow, they considered themselves ready for three days and two nights of serious trekking and laughed at my concern. Best to start cool, they said and mentioned that 15 of them had trekked in minus-50 wind-chill weather that winter.

During the days that followed, as Bill and I romped with our grandchildren, attended Easter services and dined on ham and chocolate, I found myself thinking of the voyageurs. How had they fared? Had they encountered snow? Had the temperature dropped? Had they accomplished their goal? Were they safe?

The narrative of their Easter Trek, posted later that summer on the voyageur website, had me laughing out loud. Slogging for miles through knee-deep snow and crossing flooded streams in various stages of undress to save their supplies and clothes, they were exhausted, wet and freezing by day three. A full day of slogging lay ahead. They were out of time. Out of energy. In a very un-voyageur manner, they hailed down passing snowmobilers who ferried them back to their very modern vehicle, which waited to transport them from the challenging past back into the more comfortable present.

I still had a nagging question. Why had they carried muskets when they would not be using them? I found the answer in an issue of the Minnesota/Iowa Coalition of Historic Trekkers Almanac.

"Sleeping with your shooting pouch on and your firearm between your legs not only prepares you for the unknown but is a good way to keep from flipping and flopping all night which can lead to blanket escaping."

While sleeping with a musket between one's legs seems a mighty uncomfortable way to spend a night, I'd do anything to stay under my blanket, too, especially if I were exhausted and freezing from slogging through knee-deep snow and soaking wet from fording swollen streams.

Dog Walks Cat

I returned from a month's seclusion at Norcroft in February 2003 to discover that our Schroeder household had acquired a new family member – a 60-pound, 8-year-old, sweetly disposed dog of uncertain descent.

Bill brought Shelby home from Animal Allies in Duluth in an impetuous moment of loneliness; the same place where, during one of Bill's long absences as a globetrotting consultant, I'd gone in search of a companion and acquired our very large fat cat, Ellie, also of uncertain descent.

The introduction of a dog to our household infuriated the cat. Thrusting her back into a perfect arch with every hair bristling and fangs bared, Ellie hissed and spat at Shelby. She presented a very intimidating front even to a dog Shelby's size. For weeks Ellie maintained dominance over the first floor. If Shelby followed Bill to the basement (Shelby followed Bill everywhere), Ellie held dominion over the top of the stairs to such an extent that Shelby refused to climb them unless Bill removed the cat.

Eventually, however, Ellie grew more tolerant. She even gave up control of the stairway. On cold nights, she'd sometimes snuggle next to Shelby to sleep. Shelby, for her part, converted Ellie from an indoor habitué into a lover of the out-of-doors. Walk toward any door, and you no longer walked alone – you ran a collision course with two animals who hurtled outside together, the cat flying over the dog's head in an attempt to be first.

Once outside, of course, the dog bested the cat by several hundred feet. Bill and I would race after the dog. After all, it was the dog that needed walking, not the cat. Such reasoning, however, didn't deter Ellie. She was convinced she was part of the pack and scurried after us, moving as fast as she could, belly swinging, her irate meows insisting that we "wait up, you guys."

If we stopped to wait for her, she'd slow to a dignified waddle. "Who me? Hurry after you? No way!" Shelby, anxious to get on with the walk, would trot back to the cat and nudge her. If Ellie responded too slowly, Shelby would push her from behind, an indignity Ellie was unwilling to tolerate. She'd pick up speed, for a while.

While Ellie was willing to walk in the rain, snow was another matter. Distressed to find snow outside the front door, she'd lead us to other doors, as if a snow-free scenario existed somewhere outside the house if only we could find the right exit. When snow limited her outside walks she'd thunder through the house, streak through the hallways, down the stairs and up again. Shelby, having already lunged through the snow for an hour, would lift her head and sneeze. She was not going to move unless we did.

Playing in the Mud

One of the most difficult choices we faced on moving to the North Shore was leaving the children behind. My daughter, Francesca, would give birth to a little boy the week before we moved and my son Tom's second child would arrive that November.

When we returned to visit the house for the second time – remembering the view but not what the house looked like – I stood in the sunny living room and pictured my children there. I knew they would love the house, its wide open rooms so much more spacious than their own homes; the large windows providing a soul-expanding vista of Lake Superior; the surrounding landscape a place where they could run and play and scream all they wished. I saw them coming for holidays, for vacations and simply to get away for a time from the turmoil of city living. I saw the grandchildren spending larger chunks of time with us during summer. And all that I imagined came about.

My grandchildren have been coming here from the time they were tiny tots and they still love coming. If the two younger ones are like Amber, the oldest, who is well into her teenage years yet still begs to visit, we'll have a house full of family often.

From the beginning, Amber has delighted in following deer trails through the woods, in finding that perfect fallen tree on which to sit and wait and watch. She is also our stargazer. Thomas Gregory has been skipping rocks like a champion from the time he was 3. The rocky beach is his favorite place. He spends hours scouring the beach for skipping rocks and stones with interesting patterns and colors which he lugs up to the house by the bagful.

Cassandra Mia, my youngest grandchild, has always had a decidedly different approach. She likes to get dirty ... really dirty.

I remember the early spring morning when she was 28 months old and showed this decided predilection with the greatest delight. We'd headed outdoors together to walk up the driveway to the post office. In the warm spring sun, the driveway had softened to the consistency of chocolate syrup. Deer tracks stuccoed the driveway, to which Cassandra and I added our own footprints. We matched our steps, compared our markings with those of the deer, trod lightly and left watery impressions in the mud, made great splashing jumps that left deeper impressions. We were singing and leaping when Cassandra suddenly dropped my hand and ran ahead in that wonderfully clumsy way toddlers run. She let out a yelp and dove straight down. Into the mud.

"Rock!" she shouted, shoving her pink woolen mitten into a mucky hole. Then, with the wonder and enthusiasm of a conquistador, she pushed her discovery into my face.

Now, our driveway is full of small stones and pebbles; there are thousands, millions, probably billions of them looking equally muddied and ugly in the morning thaw. Why Cassandra seized on that particular stone is beyond me. It had no distinguishing features. Rubbing it failed to reveal the subtle beauty that many of the pebbles in our driveway possess. It was not pink or pale gray or blue. It did not contain flecks of quartz or mica. It did not sport amygdaloidal bubbles nor did it contain plagioclase crystals. It did, to my adult eyes, look a bit like Mr. Potato Head.

To Cassandra, it was a treasure. We laid it carefully in the snow. She gathered up handfuls of snow and shook them onto the rock where it glittered like diamonds. We filled our hands with snow gems; let them slide through our fingers and onto our laps. We played in a treasure house of riches. We entered the kingdom of queens, sultanas and empresses. With my grandchild with me, it was easy to find the wonder hidden midst the mud and melting snow. Even the ugly drifts, graying their way to oblivion, became beautiful. Those drifts held fragile columns of ice tipped with chocolate, honeycombed caves and roofs glazed with speckled frost.

We settled onto a large rock and looked up at the sun. A chickadee landed on the spruce branch above us. When it flitted away, Cassie jumped up to imitate its bobbing flight and splattered her way back into the mud. Down the driveway she ran. I ran after her. Shluck, shluck went our boots. Tacity, tic went the mud. Plop went Cassandra into another muddy puddle. "Ukky," she said, showing me her mud-sodden mittens and laughing.

"Yucky," I grinned. But yucky was an adult's perception; not a message for a day of gems and crystals.

A Good Day to
Invade Wisconsin

"Aren't you glad we don't live in Wisconsin?" Bill asked me one spring morning as we sat sipping coffee and gazing out the window at the Lake. Sure enough the clouds were piling up on the Wisconsin side, as they seemed to do almost every morning in spring, making us wonder if Wisconsin ever had sun.

As I sat there contemplating the clouds on the Wisconsin side, giving thanks for Minnesota blue skies and enjoying our sun, Bill suddenly launched into one of his zany alter egos: Count Wilhelm Von Schickelgruber.

"And vith clouds like dat, it vould be a good day to invade Wisconsin. Ya? Dey vould never see us commin." I burst out laughing.

Our windows face Wisconsin so it is impossible not to notice that besides clouds, mirages most often appear on the Wisconsin side – sailboats that disappear for minutes then suddenly reappear, mysterious Egyptian temples that hover on the horizon to the southwest.

While Bill and I had no desire to invade Wisconsin, the armadas of diving birds mobilizing on our lakeshore that morning looked like they were considering such a tactic. There were buffleheads, goldeneyes, red-breasted and common mergansers, pied-billed, horned and red-necked grebes, and loons. They thronged the beaches, crowded onto floating logs and hugged Nessie's back. For all I knew, some husband having coffee on the Wisconsin side of the Lake and seeing fog, might, at that very moment, look toward Schroeder and tell his wife, "I wonder what

Minnesota is doing behind all that fog? Think they might be planning to invade us?" That morning it certainly looked as if invasion was just what those ducks had in mind.

Day of heavy rain and fog thick as meringue followed. Not long after the gathering of the ducks, I took our Shelby and Ellie for a sunrise walk along our Lake Superior shoreline. Had it not been for the cat, who insisted on lying down every 50 feet, I might have missed the launch of 10 or more squadrons of amphibious aircraft from the beach to the west of our home. This time it was not ducks, but hundreds of Canada geese standing in rows on my neighbor's beach, heads erect and facing Wisconsin, loud-mouthed (or should I say loud-beaked?) with excitement.

Though the geese had no intention of mimicking military maneuvers, their flight patterns reminded me of the launch of aircraft from a carrier, and I stood there awed, watching as the squawking, shrieking battalions rose skyward from the beach in units, a loose configuration of around 12 to 15 birds each, four seconds separating the launch of one group from the next. Next to take flight were the geese swimming in the Lake. Again in separate units, four seconds apart. The newly launched geese, raucous in flight, formed a loose ribbon streaming across the sky, merging into the familiar "V," unwinding as more groups raced to catch up, reforming repeatedly until they were only a blur on the horizon.

While walking back to the house, the cat lagging behind and the dog running ahead of me, I pondered what I'd witnessed. I understood that to fly freely does not mean to fly alone; there is an order and beauty in togetherness that surpasses the wonder of solitary flight. Each goose was but one unit within one species among millions on this planet; this planet but one among billions of stars in the universe; this universe just one among uncounted others and everything expressing the rapture of creation.

Back from Extinction

When, in April 2005, word came that the extinct ivory-billed woodpecker had made an appearance in a swamp in Arkansas, questions once asked by wilderness and wildlife advocates rose around dining room tables throughout the nation. What does an ivory-billed woodpecker look like? Does the male bird have a mate? How is it that such a bird should suddenly appear after more than 60 years of "extinction?" What are the factors that lead to the extinction of species?

"Lord God Bird" people called the ivory-billed woodpecker in the early days of settlement, as in "Lord God, would you look at that bird!" It was an amazing creature, huge for a woodpecker, with a large white back, brilliant red crown and an ivory-colored bill. Awe, however, couldn't protect the ivory-billed woodpecker from probable extinction; it couldn't keep hunters from killing it for trophies, it couldn't stop loggers from clear cutting its last known habitat in Louisiana. Over-logging and over-hunting, however, are not the only reasons species disappear. Exotics, species not natural to a place, also play a role.

Exotics invade and flourish, pushing native species out because they have no natural predators to control their spread. I suppose the large populations of deer that invaded the Arrowhead region of Minnesota after the clear-cutting of the white pine in the late 1800s and early 1900s, could be called exotics. The deer loved the new growth that sprouted where the great trees had fallen. The deer brought with them the brain worm that decimated the native herds of caribou and moose that once roamed the region. Today, the deer population has grown so large that even thousands of enthusiastic hunters fail to cull their numbers adequately.

During the winter of 2005, it appeared as if Highway 61 was doing its best to help with efforts to control herd size. As the snow melted, the highway exposed a winter harvest of deer killed by automobiles. It was an especially awful sight. The mangled deer hides, rib cages and hooves lay on top of what appeared to be altars of sacrifice, held aloft by the unmelted pillars of snow beneath them. While we might never see deer populations threatened, hundreds of thousands of other species – animal, plant, and insect – disappear as human populations swell the world over.

Perhaps like the fragile plants that push through our asphalt jungles, the sighting of the magnificent ivory-billed woodpecker will shatter the nonchalance with which we treat the miracles that surround us. The sighting of that ivory-billed woodpecker might never be verified, but daily we witness the tender sprouts of growth that crack the rocks on which we walk.

Seasons
of Learning

Summer

Blowdown on
Parade

Tofte, Schroeder's nearest neighbor, is just a tad larger than Schroeder, but it holds a Fourth of July bash that Schroederites wouldn't think of missing. As a newcomer, attending the Tofte parade was important to me as well. During the summer of 1999, my first summer here, I returned early from my son's 24th birthday in the Twin Cities to celebrate the Fourth with neighbors like Tom and Dory Spence (my woodcock-watching neighbor), who'd actually given up tickets to a Bob Dylan and Paul Simon concert to attend the parade.

I arrived early to find the park already crowded with optimists, no one taking seriously the overcast sky, the brisk breeze … after all, it had never rained on a Tofte parade before. As the breeze picked up and ominous green-black clouds began to hurl themselves toward the park, I saw people glance nervously at the sky, but no one moved until the first hard drops turned into a deluge. While a few hardy souls remained to keep the tents from flying into the Lake, most of us made a mad dash for the firehouse where we viewed the parade from under the mostly closed firehouse garage door. We saw only the lower portions of fire trucks and the tires and hubcaps of antique cars and trucks as they rolled past. Considering the torrents of water flooding the park, floats and marchers attempting to parade would have needed water wings. Even if the children riding decorated bikes or pulling wagons with dogs had been able to march, I doubt the parade would have lasted much longer than the $3^1/_2$ minutes it did, considering that the average length of the Tofte parade is usually around $4^1/_2$ minutes. Despite the rain, everyone seemed joyful. Children scurried after candies tossed their way by a firefighter who entered the firehouse with a box full of Jolly Ranchers and lollipops. Adults sipped liquid refreshments, beer on tap, soda and water offered for the price of a donation, and when the rain finally let up, few seemed anxious to leave.

Fireworks that night were similarly fractured. About halfway through the display, a heavy fog rolled off the Lake until we could see little more than billowing clouds illuminated with pink, green and gold. Only the sharp retorts of each fiery explosion reminded us that these were pyrotechnics. We laughed at such contrariness. So what if we couldn't see? We were together, celebrating our nation, our freedom, our place in this community, and we only had some rain and billowing fog with which to contend. Not like the storms that were roaring around Ely. Right?

It wasn't until we returned home that Mother Nature let forth with a wild celebration of her own that will imprint July 4, 1999, on North Shore minds for a long time. The storm raged through all of Cook County, washing out roads, filling basements, stranding travelers, toppling trees. Known as the Boundary Waters Blowdown, the storm roared in straight-line winds through that pristine wilderness, toppling millions of old-growth trees and devastating the land.

Neighbors called neighbors to see if everything was all right. My 86-year-old friend Bob Silver trekked down my driveway to check on my welfare because my husband was in Argentina. While the house was safe, the 18 loads of Class 5 gravel we'd added to our driveway only days before had been washed away and a huge gully at the head of the driveway made it impossible to drive in or out. Our losses were minimal compared with those suffered by others. The local web bulletin board bristled with notices of emergency situations on trails and inland roads made impassible because of floods and fallen trees, stranding and endangering hundreds of campers and travelers. Simultaneously with reports came offers to help. Then came the messages of gratitude. One message forwarded through Trinity Bethlehem Church in Grand Marais reflected my feelings as I followed reports of growing devastation and heroic efforts and rescues.

"On behalf of a group of displaced campers, I have been asked to say 'Thank you' to the Cook County community. You are a class act."

In this context, my neighbor giving up Dylan concert tickets to celebrate the Fourth of July in community makes a great deal of sense.

Hiking Trail Blues

Though Bill and I seize every free moment to explore the Superior Hiking Trail, I find it difficult to choose, when asked, which is my favorite section. Each section of the trail is distinct; even the time of day or the direction one travels on the trail can affect the trail's appearance. What one week is a narrow trail under a dense emerald canopy transforms into a ruby and topaz cloister a few days later. Though I might not be able to choose a favorite, I can definitely mention the hikes I've found most challenging.

Challenge for me comes in two forms, terrain and temperature. The hike that Bill and I took from the spur at White Sky Rock to Cascade River State Park held both challenges because that was the day temperatures in Grand Marais reached 101 degrees, and while we've hiked rougher terrain, the non-stop ups and downs of this hike brought out the worst in me.

I don't deal well with heat, or cold for that matter, but when it's hot, forget Minnesota nice. That day I suffered the added indignity of trailing a husband who climbed what seemed like never-ending slopes without stopping to catch his breath. Why did Bill have to walk so fast anyway?

With every step, I reproached myself for suggesting that we park the car at the Cascade River Park trailhead and take the shuttle to White Sky Rock rather than taking two cars, parking one at each end of the hike. Had we left a car at either end, we could have turned back much sooner. Having taken the shuttle, we had no option but to complete the 7 miles of up-and-down hiking to get back to our car.

When Bill is away, I hike in mostly mosey mode. I'm a firm proponent of the theory that moderately paced walking is as good for one's health as a fast jog. I especially like to hike this way on the Cross River trails because I can access them right from my house. There are some lovely spots that practically shout "Stop!" The Tower Overlook with sweeping views of the Lake, the rugged riverside trail with rushing waterfalls and craggy canyons, Boneye's meadow with its reflective marsh, fir-clad edges and occasional moose. It was the Cross River hike I took as a newcomer that I remember as the most challenging.

Bill was working in Texas the morning I decided to leave the house at dawn and hike the trail along the Cross River. I checked the maps and noted that I could hike up the Skou Road, take the spur trail to the Superior Hiking Trail, hike the river trail and return home via the Schroeder Tote Road. I estimated the walk would take around two hours and that I'd be back in time for breakfast. I didn't know that at the place where the Superior Hiking Trail intersected with the Schroeder Tote Road, there would be a sign saying Gasco Road, and that thinking the Schroeder Tote Road must lay ahead, I walked on … and on … and on. When I reached the Cramer Road trailhead I still had a long hike ahead of me – several miles of mostly dust and gravel on the Cramer Road. Twelve-plus miles before breakfast, without water or a map and with a moose and her calf leaving freshly made tracks ahead of me.

Was it a coincidence then, that as I finished writing this chapter, I should decide to take a "spur of the moment" hike from Silver Bay following what I remembered as the Bean and Bear Lake Loop? I planned on hiking for only an hour and didn't think it mattered if I had no water or map. I'd hiked that trail several times. When it came time to turn back, I took the wrong fork in the trail. Half an hour later, I was still looking for the spur trail back to my car. No problem, I thought. I'd just turn back and take the right fork when I found it.

Retracing my steps, however, led me onto another trail I did not recognize. I was lost. Really and truly lost. No one knew I was hiking. No one would miss me. If I stopped where I was and waited like we tell our children to do when they get lost, I could spend an awfully cold and uncomfortable night on the trail. Perhaps several. Hiking season had not yet fully begun. I kept walking and coming upon an ATV trail felt a surge of gratitude and elation. The ATV trail had to intersect with a road somewhere, and someone was more likely to drive the ATV trail than hike the Superior Hiking

Trail out of season. By that time, I was so thirsty I even considered eating the filthy melting ice on the trail. When I finally reached my car, it was 1:30 p.m. I'd started at 9 that morning.

When I e-mailed Bill, who was working in the Northwest Territories, about my adventure, Bill couldn't believe I'd done it again, that I'd gone hiking without map or water, that I'd learned so little in the 12 years we've lived here.

Jingle Dresses
and Drums

At the 1999 Rendezvous Days Powwow in Grand Portage, Bill and I climbed to the top row of the bleachers, thrilled at the opportunity to witness what until then we'd only read about – a Native American powwow.

In the arena below us, beautifully attired Native American women moved about setting up chairs and placing their children. Some wore jingle dresses with tiny decorative silver cones that glittered and tinkled, sending up a resonance like rain sticks tipped in unison. Girls flew about, making wings of their shawls, while singers and drummers gathered in the drum arbor and the honor guard and dancers gathered for the Grand Entry.

Bill and I savored our first moose burger and fry bread while a cooling breeze and moving cloud cover dissipated the hot reach of the sun. "What deliciously unhealthy food," I remarked, licking the fat from my fingers with appreciation. Only after I'd spoken did I realize that my remark might offend, especially if the listener was Native American.

I turned to the man next to me, planning to explain that my husband was a diabetic, and we usually carefully monitored what we ate, but my words died in my throat. The man next to me sat tall and regal and focused his attention on the drummers. When the Honor Guard, veterans of two World Wars, Korea and Vietnam carried the American flag into the ritual space, I felt overwhelmed with emotion. How was it possible, I wondered, that a tribe so wounded by our government could bear its flag with such obvious honor and pride?

Unfailingly polite, never alluding to the fact that he'd come for the religious significance of the celebration, my neighbor in the bleachers explained the ritual purpose of the varied songs – the drums and the chants. He told me that each festive dress worn by the dancers was unique and never to be duplicated; that an eagle feather dropped can only be retrieved by a medicine man. When the presiding Medicine Man at this powwow, Jim Windigo, gave the opening prayer, he translated its essence while revealing that he had had to relearn the Anishinaabe language as an adult.

"I lost my native tongue and culture when sent to a Christian boarding school as a child," he explained, telling me of a disastrous early adulthood transformed by a visit to a medicine man that returned him to the beliefs and language of his people. "Since then my life has been blessed," he said simply. He'd become a pilgrim, moving across the country to attend powwow celebrations nationwide.

Only later, when reading *Neither Wolf Nor Dog* by Kent Nerburn, did I realize how patient Dennis Smith had been with my questions. He'd come to the powwow as an act of spiritual ritual, and I'd thrust myself between him and that purpose.

The Big Fish Story

When Bill placed a bid on a chartered fishing trip on Lake Vermilion, he had no intention of winning said fishing trip. He was simply helping to raise the bids at a silent auction to alleviate world hunger – placing bids on seven items and periodically raising the ante. The guy bidding against him for the charter must have been doing the same because the bids kept rising. When Bill's competitor suddenly stopped, Bill held the winning bid.

Bill returned from the auction a bit shamefaced that he'd bid on a fishing trip rather than something more useful, like a year's supply of organic washing detergent. "Do you think you'd like to come?" he'd asked. While fishing has never been high on my list of priorities, I accepted. I'd never been on a fishing charter and thought it would be a lovely opportunity to experience another of Minnesota's beautiful lakes. "Go fishing with Bill," I wrote on my calendar for June 29. Then the phone rang, and I learned I had a radio interview for my book, *The Scent of God*, scheduled for the morning of June 29, so Bill invited two ardent fisher-teens to accompany him instead.

Bill set off the morning of June 29 with cold drinks, sandwiches and fruit packed in his cooler. When he returned later that night his cooler contained a trophy-sized walleye. During the first 10 minutes of his first fishing trip in eight years, Bill had landed a 9-pound, 5-ounce walleye that measured 30 inches long.

"I'd have lost that fish if the boys hadn't yelled. I was looking at the scenery, daydreaming. Completely forgot about the fishing." Bill laughed. His walleye was their only catch for the day. But what a catch.

"Did the guide fillet it for you?" I asked, having heard that guides actually do this sort of service.

"No. It's trophy size. I'm thinking of getting it mounted," he said proudly.

"You want to mount this walleye?" I asked, aghast that Bill would want to hang a stuffed fish on our walls. Dead animals, stuffed and mounted, were for other people's homes, not ours.

"Yes. Everyone said I should mount it, even gave me the name of a taxidermist in Duluth. It's the biggest fish caught today. Made the Hibbing and Duluth TV news tonight."

"There's only one reason to take a game animal's life, Bill," I replied in the most loving but forceful manner I could muster, "To give thanks and to eat it." At the time, I'd refused to note how quickly the boyish grin faded from his face, fearing we'd end up with a fish on our wall if I did. As I write this, the image of that face returns and, though the remembrance makes me sad, I'm relieved it didn't sway me that night. Much as I love my wonderful husband, I'd have hated that fish.

We ate walleye for supper that night and for breakfast the next morning and packed enough walleye into the freezer for two more meals. We don't have a mounted fish on our living room wall to attest to Bill's prowess as a fisherman, but we do have a photo of the four of them – a beaming Bill, two grinning boys and a not-so-beaming walleye.

"You ate that walleye?" trophy lovers asked when they learned what had happened to Bill's fish. "It should have been mounted."

"Mom, you didn't! You could have given it to me," my son groaned when he learned that I was the reason the walleye had not been mounted.

Yes. I sinned against the trophy fish and I feel not the slightest twinge of guilt.

Crow in Love

A knock at the front door sent me hurtling up the stairs from my basement office. I arrived at the door out of breath but found no one there. I returned to my office, puzzled but unconcerned. When the knocking recommenced, again I rushed upstairs. Once more, nothing. When the knocking continued, I climbed the stairs with less enthusiasm. My front door is mostly glass. It's easy to see who's at the door. I saw no one.

Irritated and puzzled, I opened the door and stepped outside, disturbing a large crow that propelled itself from my garden, flying to the rooftop of our detached garage. Was the crow responsible for the knocking? I waited. For several minutes the crow and I watched one another. When the crow showed no sign of moving, I headed back to my basement office. I had just settled back at my desk when the knocking started again. This time, I caught the crow in its mischief. It was pecking at the small window above the water heater in the furnace room, most likely at bugs I thought. I checked the status of bugs on the window inside. Zilch. I checked the status of bugs on the window outside. Nada. Niente.

When five days later the crow was still working at my furnace room window, I began to think that perhaps this crow had Napoleonic illusions. I'd heard of cardinals destroying a car's side-view mirrors by attacking its double image until the glass shatters. I worried about my furnace room window shattering. Then I stopped worrying. My crow did not battle. His taps were definitely not attack-mode thrusts. They were gentle. Kiss-like. I realized what was troubling my crow. He was not competing; he was in love.

"The enchanting creature you see is not the love of your life," I told him in my most careful manner. I tried not to grin at him. After all, haven't many of us made similar mistakes? "She's an illusion. A reflection of yourself." I thought of adding "you silly crow" but worried about political correctness. Who knows where crows stand on social issues.

Mr. Crow did not appear to understand my reference to illusion and reflection. He tilted his head and cawed raucously. You'll have to do better than that, he seemed to say. No way am I giving up on this babe. He shifted his licorice wings and flew back to the garage where he waited for me to leave as he'd done earlier. Moments later he was at it again. Smooching or whatever it was he was up to with my window.

I tried blocking the window with paper to cut off his reflection but he continued to peck. I stacked flowerpots to block his access. He twisted his head sideways and gave the window a lopsided kiss. Soon he'd mastered the crooked buss and the pecking grew rhythmic again.

The crow returned the following year and pecked hopefully for several days, then disappeared. Since then my window has remained unloved, unkissed, unvisited. Perhaps the crow realized his love would never be reciprocated. Perhaps he is still mourning his unrequited love. I don't know how the window feels.

Breathing
Butterflies

The small family – an infant cradled in his father's arms and a dark-haired little girl holding tightly to her mother's hand – walked straight into a mass of puddling butterflies and seemed to take it in stride, as if walking through a profusion of butterflies was something they often did.

Bill and I had headed to the Temperance River trail that afternoon, hoping to see the river in full flood. It had rained heavily earlier and the falls were most likely raging. As the family moved through the butterflies, the sun pushed through the blackened sky, turning the whirling vortex of Canadian tiger swallowtails into luminous golden petals. After the family passed, the butterflies settled back onto the muddy ground, jockeyed for puddle space, and resumed sucking moisture and minerals from the wet earth.

Seeing so many of the black-and-gold beauties at one time filled me with joy. Only once before had I seen so many butterflies gathered in one place: Lakota, Iowa, in 1996 when thousands of migrating monarchs crowded onto a tree in Bill's parents' backyard. The tree shuddered with color as the monarchs opened and closed their wings, making it look like the tree was breathing.

Bill, in his usual get-the-heart-pumping mode, had rushed past the butterflies but I lagged behind. I wanted to watch their behavior, to make certain that I'd noted all their distinguishing markings. I've found identifying butterflies difficult, testier even than learning bird song. I don't like to carry books when I hike, preferring to make mental notes, sometimes jotting things in a tiny notebook to use as references when I get home. This is not always a successful identification technique. Sometimes the butterflies I remember are not the ones I find in my reference books. I've been convinced, at times, that I've seen a species found only in the tropics. While I'd like to think I've encountered an exotic butterfly, the greater likelihood is that I've seen a moth. I bought a reference book on moths for this reason. When I am not successful at finding the name for a particular butterfly, I console myself. Did it really matter if I didn't know its name, if it was a butterfly or a humble moth, when it was so beautiful?

That afternoon I had no trouble identifying the tiger swallowtail. When swallowtails puddle, they beg to be recognized.

Schroeder's
Face-Lift

During highway renovations, Schroeder – the blip on the map few notice on their way elsewhere – gained sidewalks. Those of us who live in Schroeder wondered, "Why sidewalks?" It's not that we were averse to having sidewalks; we just weren't sure what purpose they served. My visiting sister-in-law was convinced that they were installed so I could walk safely from our driveway to the post office, several hundred feet up the road.

Besides the post office, Schroeder has a heritage center and a summer-only bakery and, on the other side of the river, an antique shop and a liquor store, but most people don't walk to these places, they drive. Schroeder's sidewalks made us wonder if the Minnesota Department of Transportation (MnDOT) knew something that we didn't, perhaps a surge in population or importance?

While the town's population and importance remains the same – it's still the town that people whip through on their way elsewhere – the town has changed. Like a balloon that suddenly deflates only to re-inflate later, the town has shrunk and expanded again. If a plastic surgeon had taken his knife to this small township of 187 residents, according to the 2000 census, the changes that have taken place could not have been more dramatic. One cut of the knife was the closing of LTV Steel's power plant and mining dock at Taconite Harbor in June 2001. On January 16, earlier in 2001, fire destroyed Northland Hardware. The following year, on March 17, 2002, fire turned the Cross River Café to rubble. Three huge losses in two years.

While the Cross River Café and Northland Hardware never arose from their ashes, Taconite Harbor had been rebirthed as Minnesota Power and Light. The Minnesota Department of Natural Resources, in cooperation with the U.S. Army Corps of Engineers and LTV Steel and Mining, created a safe harbor for small boats at the western end of the harbor. Frieda's Antiques moved into the long-empty Short Stop, and Schroeder's post office was given a brand new northwoods-style facade and a small seasonal bakery was added to the building.

One of the most stunning changes in Schroeder occurred when the highway department deeded the historic Stickney/Cross River Store (which had been slated for destruction during highway improvements) to the town, and the Schroeder Area Historical Society transformed it into the impressive Cross River Heritage Center. But I digress. Back to highway reconstruction.

Along with sidewalks, MnDOT endowed Schroeder with stone entry walls and a lovely little wayside rest where travelers can park and walk to the Cross River Falls, the only North Shore falls visible from the highway. A plaque at the wayside rest tells the story of the missionary Father Baraga who, in 1846, erected a wooden cross at the mouth of the Cross River (hence the name) in gratitude for having survived a violent storm on Lake Superior. The memorial is within walking distance from the wayside rest.

Also new with highway improvements was the Schroeder section of the Gitchi-Gami State Trail, an 86-mile, non-motorized paved trail between Two Harbors and Grand Marais running along the northeast side of the highway in Schroeder and across the impressive Temperance River Gorge.

While Schroeder might still be the town that you'll miss if you blink while on your way elsewhere, you could stop and pay a visit. There's plenty of parking, a great view of the Cross River and Falls, a Heritage Center and the Baraga Memorial. While you're at it, mail a postcard at the P.O., have a donut and coffee, and don't forget to use the sidewalks.

Unlocking the Mysteries

Five years after moving to Lake Superior's North Shore, I finally learned to use a key. Not an ordinary key, mind you. This key opened doors to plant identification, and I learned how to use it during a Naturalist Weekend workshop at Sugarloaf Cove Interpretive Center at the far west end of Cook County in Schroeder.

Though I'd always appreciated nature's beauty, it wasn't until I moved to the North Shore that I wanted to live in, rather than on, the land. I began spending every minute I could outdoors, even carrying my meals down to the Lake to eat when the weather allowed. Seated next to Lake Superior's icy waters, surrounded by soaring ring-billed gulls and diving mergansers and lovely purple bell-shaped flowers peeking from nests of fine grass, I wanted to learn their names. I used my guidebooks, as many of us do, by looking for the pictures that most resembled what I'd seen and avoiding the complex keys. After my naturalist workshop at Sugarloaf, this was no longer the case.

On my very first day at Sugarloaf, by learning how to use "the key system" in *Newcomb's Wild Flower Guide*, I worked my way step-by-step through the genus Salix, past wondrous words like glabrous and glaucous (wrap your tongue around those) to the species specific bebbiana, more commonly known as Bibbs Willow, or Beaked Willow. Soon all of us in the naturalist class were deep into reference books.

We checked the pattern of leaf edges, the way those leaves were attached to their stems, the shape of the leaves, the kind of blossoms, the color and number of the petals. The keys enabled us to identify everything we found during our hikes through varied terrain, from rocky shoreline to inland bog. With whoops of joy we identified the tiny arctic eyebright (*Euphrasia hudsoniana*), miniature goldenrod (*Solidago ptarmicoidis*) and dainty brook lobelia (*Lobelia kalmii*). No more paging through books looking for pictures.

That was the plan. Human nature being human nature, I sometimes find it's just easier to look for those photos. I check the keys when all else fails.

Confessions of a Dawn/Dusk Dog Walker

On the two occasions when I've followed fox tracks on a beach, the fox itself has leaped from hiding like a red-tailed comet. This happened once in Old Woman Bay, Ontario. The second time was at dawn right here on our beach at home. For the latter sighting, I have our dog, Shelby, to thank. I'd always enjoyed hiking, but until Shelby entered our lives I preferred taking those jaunts by myself. I never dreamed that I'd actually look forward to struggling out of bed at 5 a.m. to walk a dog.

Though Shelby was very thoughtful about where she relieved herself (always off the road in tall grass or woods), she didn't view being let outside as an invitation to take care of nature, as do most other dogs. Instead, she'd wait patiently at the door for one or the other of us to accompany her when she needed to "go." That meant a lot of walks in all kinds of weather.

In the beginning – when I was still miffed that Bill had brought Shelby home without consulting me – I left this necessary dog walking to my husband. It was a "he got her, he can walk her" mentality. I changed my mind the dusky evening Bill returned from one of those walks to ask the name of the bird "that makes that crazy buzzing noise."

For several years I'd traipsed over to my neighbor Dory's field to try to catch a woodcock performing its courtship ritual. Bill's casual remark informed me that I could have seen the whole event in the privacy of my own driveway. The next evening, I walked Shelby. I wanted to encounter that woodcock myself. And there, as Bill indicated, was the woodcock. Even Shelby sat entranced as we watched the stocky long-beaked little fellow puff out its chest, turn this way and that, while uttering its nasal "peent." We heard it sputter into the sky with a trilling of wings, watched its batlike swoop through our woods in a wide circling arc, its swirling twittering descent to the driveway barely two feet away. Shelby and I viewed nine or more of these exhibitions before continuing our walk. From then on in June, even if Bill was home, dog-walking at dusk became my prerogative.

Late night walks were a different matter. On one exceedingly dark and moonless night, Shelby, who didn't bark without a lot of encouragement (barking is one of my least favorite things Bill taught her to do) stopped short, uttered a soft growl, then shot toward the house. Bill raced down the driveway after her, convinced that whatever Shelby sensed in the woods was probably not another dog.

The next morning, the three of us set out for a walk at dawn along the lakeshore, leaving Ellie behind because the four bald eagles that accompanied us might have considered her a tempting morsel.

As we walked, more eagles appeared until I'd counted 10 flying with us. We'd never seen so many eagles in such close proximity to one another or to us. We knew why the eagles were there when we rounded a bend on the beach and encountered a deer carcass lying on the rocky shore, half in, half out of the water. It was obviously fresh kill, the internal cavity still bloody, half the rib cage ripped away, probably by whatever it was that Shelby sensed the night before.

Both Shelby and Ellie our fat cat died several years ago, within months of one another. Bill and I were too grief stricken to replace them. Two years later, however, the longing for a pet began to niggle the back of my mind. We adopted a 14-year-old cat, Candy, who likes to type and will paw Bill's closed eyelids to check if he's awake. We stuck with cats. Cats don't need to be walked at night.

Paddling with the
Dragons

Me? A dragon boat racer? You bet!

When I was asked to join a team of dragon boat racers for the second annual Grand Marais Dragon Boat Racing Festival in August 2005, I decided to go for it. The "no experience necessary" factor convinced me. With only one practice session prior to the race, how hard could it be? I knew how to paddle.

On the morning before the actual race, 19 members of the Black Iris Productions dragon boat team – most of us first-timers – gathered under the Black Iris tent on the east side of the west bay. We were there to learn how to race a dragon boat and to practice what we learned. Before we could begin, however, we needed to appoint a steersperson and a drummer. As one of the oldest paddlers (age 65 at the time), I volunteered as drummer, but Diane Fitzgerald's shoulder problems edged me out. Tess, with recent military experience, volunteered as steersperson. Tess took to the role as if she'd been leading dragon boat teams forever. First, we needed to stretch, she said. One vigorous stretching session later, Tess steered us down to the docks at the Coast Guard Station and settled us according to size and weight into one of the long dragon boats.

"OK, ladies!" shouted the petite blonde coach assigned our crew. "Man your paddles. Now stroke. Stroke. Stroke. Remember! Arms straight. Keep that 'A'."

We thrust our paddles high, then plunged them into the water. Up, down, up down. Pistons we became, but it wasn't good enough for our pretty trainer who could not have been more than 20 years old. From a championship Canadian team, she expected more of us neophytes.

"Your hands should be IN the water," she challenged. "Dig those paddles deep; then pull. Think of mud. You are thrusting mud."

For an hour and a half we sweated and lunged and pushed our boat through the waters of the Grand Marais west bay. My shoulders burned. My arms trembled. My heart pounded. Deceived by the "no experience necessary" criteria for volunteers, I'd let the summer pass without preparing. I didn't lift weights. I didn't go canoeing. Heck. There were days when I didn't even stretch. When the practice session finally ended, I staggered from the boat toward my car with Tess' final warning echoing in my ears.

"Don't let that lactic acid collect in your muscles. Otherwise you're going to be really stiff tomorrow."

Tomorrow? What about today? Even unlocking the car seemed beyond me that afternoon. I did, however, make it home. Once safely in the house, I gulped a couple of Advil, pulled out my sticky mat and did my best to stretch.

On Saturday, the day of the races, the west bay was not the tranquil harbor it had been the day before. The wind blew and the water roiled. As we paddled across the bay toward the starting point, our boat rose and fell on the swells. At times we rose so high we found ourselves paddling air. At other times, the boat rocked sideways and water sloshed over the side.

"Listen, crew!" shouted Diane, our valiant drummer, who was seated on a narrow little stool in the bow of the boat, with only the drum to anchor her feet. "If I think I'm going over the side, I'm hanging on with both hands. Forget the drum."

The size of the swells frightened us and our paddling lost its synchronicity. From her steersperson position in the stern of the boat, Tess roared, "These boats don't capsize. Keep paddling!" And so we did.

"We can do this, crew!" Tess shouted.

"We can do this!" we shouted back. We chanted, we counted strokes, we cried "pull, pull, pull," and we hadn't even begun to race. We were still on our way to the starting line. But we were primed. We were ready. We came in second to last.

During the relays that followed, paired with the champion Canadian team Free West, we learned what it really meant to paddle. The Canadians' arms formed perfect As with their paddles. They did not bend their arms but paddled with their bodies, bending low over their knees and using their legs to bounce up for the next stroke.

Up, down, up, down, the drummer shouted, and up and down we went. As we reached the dock, we raised our paddles in a V and yelped with joy. We'd lost again, but we were high with exuberance. We'd done it and no one had died.

My racing companion, Marcia, leaned over to ask if I would be racing next year.

"Sure," I chortled. "Next year I'll be ready. I'm going to start working out ... sometime."

Next year I attended the races as an observer, as I've done every year since.

My Little Red Writing Shed

During the summer of 2006, shortly after my book *The Scent of God* was published, the little red writing shed where I wrote much of that book arrived at our house from Norcroft. After 14 years of nurturing hundreds of women authors, Norcroft was closing. Its founder and guardian angel, Joan Drury, could no longer support such a big project. She was putting the property up for sale and finding takers for the writing sheds.

I'd been especially blessed by Norcroft. Though Norcroft was officially closed during winter, Joan made the lodge available to writers who could live there alone for a full month at a time. I spent two Februarys this way, tucked within its blessed space, surrounded by deep snow, silent spruce trees and an icy Lake Superior. I'd also acted as caretaker when the director was on holiday, living in the small cottage next to the lodge and doing the shopping and groundskeeping for the residents.

Norcroft provided a beautiful lodge that housed four residents at a time, supplying each resident with a shed of her own in which to work. Joan Drury, an award-winning writer herself, was convinced that in seclusion and silence, women would tap into their creative genius. She was not mistaken. Her bookshelves are filled with autographed copies of the books that took shape in those writing sheds.

Prior to my experience at Norcroft, I'd done the writer-in-the-coffee shop thing that seems to inspire some writers. I'd written in parks, on buses, during lunch breaks at work, risen early and gone to bed late to write, but at Norcroft I wrote more in two weeks than I'd written in two years elsewhere.

The writing shed delivered to my home in 2006 has since become my mini-Norcroft. When I head to my writing shed every morning, I leave the house and all its distractions behind to focus on one thing only: my writing. I have no telephone or Internet service in the shed to distract me. I've spent so much time in my shed's warm embrace writing that locals think I've moved.

"Are you visiting?" they ask when they encounter me elsewhere. No, I tell them. Not visiting. Just writing.

The Attack
of the Slugs

My writing shed sits on what was once our vegetable garden. Our vegetable garden provided everything a writing shed needs: a level space, good drainage, sunshine and a view of the Lake. We didn't yield the garden to make room for the shed. We'd abandoned the garden a year earlier.

If you consider six inches of rocky soil an adequate gardening medium, you might think gardening on Lake Superior's shoreline less of a challenge than Bill and I found it. Besides poor soil, our gardening difficulties have been complicated by critters both large and small, winds from the Lake and the north, and a miserably short growing season.

To garden on the North Shore of Minnesota, you need determination, raised beds and maybe a micro-climate or two. We were deficient on all counts, save for the raised beds, which we could and did build. We hauled in enough railroad ties to build a 12-by-12-foot box, dumped several truckloads of black earth into the resulting frame and enriched that black earth with organic compost, peat moss and manure.

We situated our raised bed on the south side of our detached garage so it could get whatever sun was available and would have some protection from north winds. We surrounded our garden with 10-foot-high deer fencing. We planted cool weather crops: sweet and snap peas, green beans, mesclun and leaf lettuce, spinach, beets, potatoes, carrots, broccoli, cabbage, peppers, cucumbers, cilantro, parsley and basil.

Our efforts to grow corn and tomatoes were doomed from the start – too much wind, too little sun, too little growing time – but everything else thrived, especially the peas, beans, cilantro and lettuce. Our garden flourished that first year. From late spring through early summer, we weeded and picked and dined on produce from our own garden.

The second year the garden produced, but with a smaller yield. We amended the soil with more manure and compost before replanting the third year. The garden had just started to bloom when two whitetail deer leaped the fence and ate their fill of tender blooms, demolishing the fence when leaving. Then the slugs arrived. Filling shallow tins with beer, dumping the drowned slugs every few days and refilling the tins with beer seemed to help. I set out planks of wood and scraped their squatter populations into salted water. The following year, the slugs returned with a vengeance, determined to exact retribution for their so cruelly departed brethren. My beer and board efforts to control the slimy creatures could not compete with their reproductive agility. I harvested more slugs than produce. We abandoned the garden mid-season and started buying organic at the local co-op.

It was probably not a good idea, then, to read Barbara Kingsolver's book *Animal, Vegetable, Miracle: A Year of Food Life*, as I've just done. She describes becoming a *locavore* – one who eats only seasonal, locally grown foods – with such delectable words that I'm almost convinced we should give the garden another try.

That would mean, of course, building another raised bed to replace the one now hosting my writing shed and contending with the same difficulties that confronted us last time we tried. Hmmm. Maybe a greenhouse is a better idea. Bill has often dreamed of having a greenhouse. Perhaps when he retires. Meanwhile, I'll leave gardening to the experts and get my exercise in the woods.

Our Backyard Labyrinth

Four years ago, during the same summer that my writing shed arrived, my husband built a labyrinth in our front yard. A labyrinth seemed like a natural complement to the walking paths Bill had already built, the meditation benches he'd placed along those paths, the hermitage-like shed where I write and our inspiring view of the Lake. When Bill called our home "Beryl's monastery," he wasn't joking. I think of it as "the monastery that Bill built."

We were introduced to labyrinths when we made a weekend retreat at the McCabe Center, a retreat house in Duluth run by Benedictine nuns. A physical metaphor for life's journey, a labyrinth is a mini-pilgrimage leading purposefully, in tight concentric circles or spirals, toward the center and back again to the beginning.

The experience of walking the labyrinth at McCabe convinced Bill that we needed a labyrinth of our own. As soon as he got home, he headed straight to his computer, downloaded labyrinth designs and went to work. When I returned from a book tour the following week, we had our very own labyrinth. To build it, Bill had culled fallen birch logs from our woods, cut them into 8-inch lengths, split them and used them to border the labyrinth path, which he filled with woodchips. He worked all day, every day, for a week to finish the project.

Ours is not a traditional labyrinth such as those found in the ancient cathedrals in Europe. The labyrinth Bill built conforms to the topography of our land. The shape, the ruts and ridges of the field in front of our home define our labyrinth. It looks quite pretty tucked among the grasses and wildflowers, its meandering spirals bordered with split logs and filled with wood chips, with Lake Superior providing a gorgeous blue backdrop.

Bill and I walk the labyrinth often. We walk it as a meditative practice, but also when we need a break from work or to resolve one problem or another. The feeling of centeredness it elicits helps clear our minds and calm our spirits. Evening is our favorite time to walk the labyrinth. Though Shelby and Ellie are no longer with us, I often think of the way they'd cross borders to wait for us as we rounded the next loop. They didn't need a labyrinth; they'd come only to keep us company. Our pets already lived in the center.

A Flash of
Tangerine

I'd just talked myself up the final section of one very long, steep ascent on the Superior Hiking Trail when a flash of tangerine flew past me and disappeared into a thicket.

Wanting to see if the bird would re-emerge, I stood as still as I could, hoping it would think I was a tree. This ruse must have succeeded because in less than a minute, the bird popped its black head from the shrubs and, after a careful look round, fluttered back into the clearing.

It was a tiny jewel of a bird, its colors onyx black with tangerine bands on and under its wings and tail. As I watched, it hopped over and onto branches, occasionally flashing its brilliantly colored wings and tail. I'd never seen one of these whatever-it-wases before and wondered if Bill had seen it. It was too lovely to miss. When the bird finally disappeared, I hurried to catch up with my husband, encountering on the way a young girl and her parents coming in the other direction.

"There's a gorgeous bird up ahead. Black and bright orange," I told them.

"Yes, we saw it, too, on the way up," the father replied. "A redstart."

A redstart? They must be mistaken, I thought. That bird was not red. It had the brightest orange flares I'd ever seen. When I caught up with Bill I asked if he had seen the tiny bird. He hadn't.

On the way back to the car, Bill was once again ahead of me. As usual, I was noting the first blooming bunchberries, clintonia in full bloom, sarsaparilla, and a rhizomatous clubmoss that clambered over a large boulder like a fuzzy green rope. And though I wasn't that far behind Bill, the redstart again reappeared and flash-danced in front of me. Perhaps it had performed for Bill as well.

"Did you see the bird this time, Bill?" I asked when I caught up with him. I'd wanted so badly for him to see that lovely little creature. He shook his head no.

And yes. It was a redstart. My *Peterson* and *Audubon* guides verified it. The "All about Birds" website describes the redstart as "a boldly patterned warbler of second-growth woods, the American Redstart frequently flashes its orange and black wings and tail to flush insect prey from foliage."

Now that's something to ponder the next time a redstart flashes across my path.

A Summer Case
of Spring Fever

Summer solstice 2007 was over; the stilts and puppets and masks from the celebrations packed away, but we'd not yet seen spring. Perhaps that's why spring still coursed through my blood when I discovered blue-eyed grass growing on both sides of our driveway.

"If you aren't the most beautiful little things," I gushed. "Look at you, sprouting here with your six blue-purple petals and bright gold centers."

While I've been known to cry "Congratulations!" to winter wrens after exceptionally glorious songs and talk to trees and flowers, I don't usually burble. This cluster of bright blue-eyes was an exception. Blue-eyed grass is one of my favorite flowers, but until then I'd seen them only occasionally. Certainly never in such profusion as I did that morning. I glanced around, hoping no one had seen me. (Yes, I'm confessing to you in the written word, but you didn't see me singing to those flowers, did you?) Resolved to refrain from further prattling, I hurried back to the house for my camera. Blue-eyed grass is notoriously fussy about lighting so it's important to take their pictures immediately, which I did.

The cluster of blue-eyed grass was the first of the encounters that excited me that afternoon. After saying goodbye to the grass, I headed up to the Cascade River to take photos of the rampaging cataracts triggered by the heavy rains we'd been having all month.

I'd done the loop, visited each overlook to gape at the roiling water, stopped on the bridge to take more photos of the cascades, then headed back down the east side of the river to the car. On the way, I passed an exceptionally large mat of bunchberry blossoms tumbling over the mosses and into the woods. Another blanket of these flowers edged the trail bordering the river. I looked to see if there were more of these blanketing blooms, delighted that cool weather and rain had generated such a profusion of flowers. As I started to take a photo of the bunchberry blooms, something pink drew my eyes in the opposite direction. I stopped, astounded. Right there, sheltered under a white spruce, a stemless lady's slipper shone translucent in the dappled light.

I'd seen lady's slippers in the wild only twice before. Once when my wild-flower friend, Virginia, and I went in search of the yellow lady's slippers growing in the Grand Portage area. The other sighting was the showy (or queen's) lady's slipper adorning the swamplands between the Sugarloaf and Cramer Roads. On the Cascade River trail, I encountered not only one lady's slipper, but an entire family of them, clustered in groups or flourishing by themselves. I didn't talk to these beauties. I remembered just in time that I was on a public trail, not a private driveway. I knelt instead and took their pictures.

A Best Kept Secret

August is berry-picking time here in Minnesota's Arrowhead. Bill and I have lived here for 12 berry seasons, but in all that time, no one has ever told us where to find even one wild blueberry patch. Longtime resident berry pickers up here guard the whereabouts of these blueberry patches with determination, passing the secret from one generation to the next, but rarely, if ever, sharing that secret with others. These blueberry pickers return from berry-picking excursions with ice-cream pails filled to overflowing with the tiny, succulent fruits. When I've asked where they find them, they've told me that the berries can be found "up there" and wave their hands vaguely in the direction of the hills. They will even go so far as to tell me that back roads and burned over and rocky areas are good places to look. They'll bake blueberry pies for church and flower club gatherings, but divulge the actual locations of the blueberry patches? Never!

Not that Bill and I have felt deprived. The masses of wild raspberries lining our driveway keep us busy enough. There have, however, been two occasions when we've gone hiking and stumbled unexpectedly into as-yet unharvested blueberry patches.

Several years ago, while hiking a rather lengthy section of the Superior Hiking Trail, we topped a rocky hill and were greeted by what might have been a good half acre of berries. There were so many berries that the hillside looked blue. Having no containers (no way were we going to empty our water bottles when we had miles to go) and feeling hot and sweaty, that hillside spelled paradise. We spent close to 20 minutes stuffing ourselves. I must have done an especially good job of downing berries because it wasn't long after we'd resumed hiking that I grew so dizzy I had to clutch a tree to stay upright.

"A sugar low," Bill surmised knowledgeably. "You ate too many berries on an empty stomach. Your blood sugar surged and then dipped precipitously." Oh sure, I thought. I'm not the one with diabetes here.

"I'm fine," I assured him. We finished the hike without any further episodes.

Because it was an especially long hike, we'd parked one car at the trail end and another at the beginning. That way we could drive back to the trailhead where we'd left the other car, rather than retracing our steps. I was driving the Subaru with Bill following in the truck when the blueberries exacted payment. To say I had a hard time staying awake is to put it mildly. Bill flashed his lights at me in warning. I'm fine, I waved back. When I swerved over the center line, he blared his horn at me and told me to pull over and walk around. The fact that I am writing this article testifies to our safe arrival home. I learned my lesson. Empty stomachs and too many blueberries spell trouble.

My 9-year-old grandson Tommy was with us on the Superior Hiking Trail the day we encountered another patch of blueberries. This time we actually had containers with us. I'd packed a picnic lunch to eat on the trail: lemonade, sandwiches, nuts and apples. The cups we'd used for our lemonade made perfect blueberry receptacles.

"Gosh, you pick fast," Bill commented as I dumped handful after handful of berries into my cup, twice as fast as he did and probably four times faster than Tommy, who definitely ate more than he picked.

"That's because I'm picking, not eating," I responded rather snidely. From then on we've made a point of hiking that trail in August, always with containers and always surprised to find that we've beaten the campers and the bears to the harvest.

If you were to ask where we get our blueberries, I would tell you that you can't drive to our blueberry patches. You will have to go hiking. I will wave my arm vaguely toward the hills and say, "Oh, they're up there. Somewhere."

I've been here 12 years. I've learned my lesson well.

A Grief Absorbed

Our lives on Lake Superior have been as magical as the blooming of the genie from Aladdin's freshly polished lamp, but we've been luckier than Aladdin. We've had more than three wishes fulfilled.

As I started selecting the stories with which to weave *A View of the Lake*, the telling transformed into "a view *from* the Lake." It became clear that the Lake and its environs had mentored me into an awareness that the greatest miracles are often the smallest and least recognized.

There is one story, however, that I have waited until now to share. I wrestled for months about how I could include this story without letting it engulf the rest of the book. Though it happened early in our stay here, placing it within the narrative would have colored the flow of the book, would have necessitated balancing subsequent stories against the story that threatened to destroy the joy we'd found in our view of the Lake.

Early Tuesday morning, September 18, 2001, one week to the day after the Twin Towers in New York went down in flames and after Francesca had driven five hours from Minneapolis to be with me, my beautiful 24-year-old daughter was shot and killed in a north Minneapolis duplex where she'd sought shelter. Her death – an unresolved case in the homicide files of the Minneapolis Police Department – tore our lives wide open, engulfing us in grief as we'd never experienced it. You haven't seen much of Francesca in these stories because, though her visits to our home on Lake Superior were joyful, they were but brief interludes in a concerto of dissonance. The only time we weren't worrying about her was when she was here.

When Francesca was little, I'd hear other parents grouse about their rebellious teens and think how lucky I was. My little girl would never give me that kind of trouble. She was so bright and loving, thoughtful and generous. If I worried, it was about her attachment to home, the way she seemed to prefer my company to that of her peers. When she began middle school, she wept every morning for months, begging to stay home. I had little patience with her tears: I was going through the end of a relationship, struggling to make ends meet, working full-time, caring for an elderly mother and trying to get my college degree. When the crying finally stopped, my spirits lifted. I didn't learn for months that Francesca wept because a new group of "friends" at middle school had introduced her to alcohol, and she didn't know how to tell me. Afraid of hurting me, of causing more suffering than I already had, she kept silent and tried to cope on her own. From alcohol, it was but a short step to marijuana and from there to most every drug conceivable. Therapy and treatment centers could not stop her downward slide. Though others saw her as charismatic, funny, beautiful and bright, she believed herself a failure. Two years of sobriety during the early years of her son's life disintegrated when she and her partner separated.

When Francesca appeared at our home on September 11, 2001, she came not only to tell me she loved me and to apologize for all the grief she'd caused, but to ask if she could return home for a while. She was frightened. I suggested she not return to the city if she was that frightened, but she said she had to give notice at work and gather her things. She never made it back.

I do not know whether Francesca would have found the safety and healing she sought here, but I do know that she loved this place. I think the vast expanse of Lake and land soothed her wild spirit. I remember her every visit, there were so few of them. I see her running, arms flung wide open, down a hillside toward the Lake the first time she visited us. Memories of Francesca reverberate each time I cross the section of the Superior Hiking Trail where we encountered the fresh tracks of a large moose in the wet earth, and my daring daughter refused to let me go any farther. I hear her gasp every time I drive past Cut Face Creek on the way to Grand Marais – the sweep of Lake and land below us taking her breath away. I see her flying back toward me, camera in hand, having had a close encounter with a deer as she rounded the side of the house. I have that photo. The deer looks as startled as Fran felt. On September 12 of that fateful year, we hiked to Devil's Kettle and dined at Naniboujou Lodge. Fran looks so beautiful in the photos I took that day, happy and, yes, healthy. Was she already on the road to recovery? The autopsy reports say that she was a healthy, well-nourished young woman – a diagnosis not often applied to addicts.

Francesca's ashes lie buried on a knoll overlooking Lake Superior. It is a beautiful spot with an incredible view. I know she'd have loved it. A large birch towers over her grave – a birch that grew from the rotting trunk of a mighty white pine. It is not the same tree that Bob Silver showed me in his photos, but it is a very old tree. Already it shows signs of the death that will eventually strip its branches. I've promised myself that this birch will stand until it falls on its own and returns to earth the life that sustained it. Perhaps in its dying, this birch, like the white pine that nourished it, will give birth to another tree as mighty and beautiful.

Burying Francesca's ashes here makes our home on Lake Superior even more sacred. The land that holds her ashes, breathes her wild spirit.

Our Lake Superior home, a place of so much joy, has also become a place of many tears. As I grieved my daughter's tormented life and violent death, the lakeshore sheltered me, provided a place where I could cry aloud in anguish and pound the earth in rage without alerting the neighbors. This landscape did not judge my tears or exact more than I was able to give. This land is infinitely patient, it understands the time it takes for life to spring again from death. For more than two years, the land waited as I grappled with darkness; the land and the Lake waited until I was ready to leave the bleakness of winter and journey once again into the glory of spring, the shared hope of summer and the radiance of fall.

I can see Francesca's grave from my kitchen window. Every day I cross the rustic bridge that leads to the knoll where she lies and I greet her. I sit on the big cedar swing built by our good neighbor Bob, the same swing where Francesca and I sat the week before she died, her small hand tucked in mine as we talked about hope and forgiveness. I am grateful for the belief that in dying Francesca attained the wholeness for which she longed. My girl is at peace and I no longer have to worry about her safety.

When Bill is home, he joins me on the swing. We sit there together holding hands and gazing at the view that drew us here, smelling the scent of the balsam poplar wafting round us and watching the geese flying above us like noisy, demented teens. So much has transpired and we are grateful for all of it. The growth that occurs in the sunlight begins in the darkness beneath the earth.

Heart of Stone

On the day we first saw the place we've called "home" for the past 12 years, I found a heart-shaped, palm-sized stone on the Lake Superior beach our home overlooks.

Aside from its shape, there was nothing particularly beautiful about this stone – it was gray, without a hint of the pinks, blues and lavenders of the other rocks surrounding it. This heart-shaped stone, however, seemed to promise change, the new beginning for which I hadn't even known that I'd longed until I saw this place.

Already bewitched by the unbroken view of Lake Superior, its ledgerock shoreline and the wooded knolls of its surrounding landscape, I assigned the rock the role of talisman and tucked it into my pocket. That afternoon, as Bill and I sat on the beach listening to the waves and warmed by the sun, it seemed that we had found the place we wanted to make our home.

Lake Superior unleashed an immense geyser of longing within me. It offered solitude, incredible beauty and inner fulfillment. In this remote location, I could live the deep interior life that had once drawn me to a monastic order and for which I still ached. Perhaps I could even become the writer I knew I was.

When we left the shore, I took the stone back to the Twin Cities with me. That night I fell asleep with the stone in my hand. When I woke the next morning, my stone seemed to emanate warmth and comfort. I found myself holding it as I meditated, and the certainty grew that on the Lake I would learn all that I needed to know. Each night as I retired, I folded the rock within my right hand and prayed we'd find a home in the place from which it had come.

For the last 12 years, from the large windows that encompass three sides of the house, I watch Lake Superior assume one or another of her many faces – from reflective nun to raging virago. She's a strict and sometimes hard mother, but her welcome is as wide as her expanse is vast.

Living in the Lake's immediate presence, I've been encouraged to respond to life as a child does: fully and without reservation. That child is busy. She's watching, listening and learning. Her mentors are the Lake, the land, its denizens, the seasons and the sky.

It is strange that once we moved, I forgot my rock. I didn't think of it until months later while taking a course on writing about place. Since Francesca died, I often comb the beach looking for more heart-shaped rocks which I gather to tuck among the pink, gray and blue cobbles above her ashes. I do not know what happened to the rock that drew us here. Perhaps in fulfilling its promise, it melded back into the landscape. Perhaps it found its way to Francesca's grave. Wherever that heart-shaped rock lies, I carry its imprint on my heart. It speaks of love and of gratitude for everything that has happened to us here.

In 1998, Bill and I fell in love with a view, bought the land that encompassed it and fell body and soul into the heart of a miracle. It's been said that gratitude is the most perfect prayer. If this is so, then my husband and I live that prayer daily.

About the Author

William D. Christ

Beryl Singleton Bissell came to the Big Lake after a lifetime of adventures and heartaches.

She was born in New Jersey, raised there and in Puerto Rico, and, when she was 18, joined the Poor Clare Sisters of the Second Order of St. Francis in a cloistered monastery in New Jersey. Her life took an unanticipated turn when she took time away from the monastery to care for her ailing father in Puerto Rico and fell in love with a priest, Vittorio Bosca Pelle. Both of them would leave their church positions – though not their church or their passion for God – and marry. Their children Tomas and Francesca were still toddlers when Vittorio died of pancreatic cancer five years later.

Beryl eventually moved her small family to the Twin Cities and later began working for Milkweed Editions in Minneapolis, first as intern coordinator and office manager and later as associate development director. Between her work at Milkweed and her connection to The Loft program in Minneapolis, she realized and honed her writing skills. Her popular memoir, *The Scent of God* (Counterpoint, 2006) grew from that realization.

When Beryl and Bill Christ, a Lutheran pastor and an international change management consultant, met on a blind date, they knew they'd be spending the rest of their lives together. Then, on something of a whim and now the basis for this memoir, the couple became owners of property on Lake Superior and began a new, intriguing life chapter. Beryl became a freelance writer and a columnist for the *Cook County News Herald* in Grand Marais, Minnesota, while for a time Bill continued his consultant work with frequent commuting.

Another tragedy would befall the family when Beryl's precious daughter Francesca was murdered in 2001. As any parent who loses a child knows, the world develops an undercoat of sadness that forever tints even the brightest of joys.

But despite the losses she's endured, Beryl's faith remains strong and joy and love continue to dominate a life lived for well over a decade on the shores of the mighty and mystical Lake Superior.

From Lake Superior Port Cities Inc.
www.lakesuperior.com

Lake Superior Magazine
A bimonthly, regional publication
covering the shores along Michigan,
Minnesota, Wisconsin and Ontario

Lake Superior Travel Guide
An annually updated mile-by-mile guide

**Lake Superior, The Ultimate Guide to the
Region – Second Edition**
Softcover: ISBN 978-0-942235-97-5

Hugh E. Bishop:
The Night the Fitz Went Down
Softcover: ISBN 978-0-942235-37-1

**By Water and Rail: A History of Lake
County, Minnesota**
Hardcover: ISBN 978-0-942235-48-7
Softcover: ISBN 978-0-942235-42-5

Haunted Lake Superior
Softcover: ISBN 978-0-942235-55-5

Haunted Minnesota
Softcover: ISBN 978-0-942235-71-5

Bonnie Dahl:
**Bonnie Dahl's Superior Way,
Fourth Edition**
Softcover: ISBN 978-0-942235-92-0

Joy Morgan Dey, Nikki Johnson:
Agate: What Good Is a Moose?
Hardcover: ISBN 978-0-942235-73-9

Daniel R. Fountain:
**Michigan Gold,
Mining in the Upper Peninsula**
Softcover: ISBN 978-0-942235-15-9

Marvin G. Lamppa:
Minnesota's Iron Country
Softcover: ISBN 978-0-942235-56-2

Daniel Lenihan:
**Shipwrecks of
Isle Royale National Park**
Softcover: ISBN 978-0-942235-18-0

Betty Lessard:
Betty's Pies Favorite Recipes
Softcover: ISBN 978-0-942235-50-0

James R. Marshall:
**Shipwrecks of Lake Superior,
Second Edition**
Softcover: ISBN 978-0-942235-67-8

**Lake Superior Journal:
Views from the Bridge**
Softcover: ISBN 978-0-942235-40-1

Howard Sivertson
**Driftwood:
Stories Picked Up Along the Shore**
Hardcover: ISBN 978-0-942235-91-3

**Schooners, Skiffs & Steamships:
Stories along Lake Superior's Water
Trails**
Hardcover: ISBN 978-0-942235-51-7

Tales of the Old North Shore
Hardcover: ISBN 978-0-942235-29-6

The Illustrated Voyageur
Hardcover: ISBN 978-0-942235-43-2

**Once Upon an Isle:
The Story of Fishing Families
on Isle Royale**
Hardcover: ISBN 978-0-962436-93-2

Frederick Stonehouse:
**Wreck Ashore: United States
Life-Saving Service,
Legendary Heroes of the
Great Lakes**
Softcover: ISBN 978-0-942235-58-6

Shipwreck of the Mesquite
Softcover: ISBN 978-0-942235-10-4

Haunted Lakes (the original)
Softcover: ISBN 978-0-942235-30-2

Haunted Lakes II
Softcover: ISBN 978-0-942235-39-5

Haunted Lake Michigan
Softcover: ISBN 978-0-942235-72-2

Haunted Lake Huron
Softcover: ISBN 978-0-942235-79-1

Julius F. Wolff Jr.:
**Julius F. Wolff Jr.'s
Lake Superior Shipwrecks**
Hardcover: ISBN 978-0-942235-02-9
Softcover: ISBN 978-0-942235-01-2

www.lakesuperior.com
1-888-BIG LAKE (888-244-5253)
Outlet Store: 310 E. Superior St., Duluth, MN 55802